Collected Poems

NORMAN CAMERON

Collected Poems

and Selected Translations

EDITED BY
WARREN HOPE
AND
JONATHAN BARKER

Anvil Press Poetry

Published in 1990
by Anvil Press Poetry Ltd
69 King George Street London SE10 8PX

Copyright © Jane Aiken Hodge 1990
Introduction copyright © Jonathan Barker 1990
'Norman Cameron 1905–1953' copyright © Warren Hope 1990

This book is published
with financial assistance from
The Arts Council

Designed and composed by Anvil
Photoset in Bembo by Wordstream
Printed and bound in Great Britain
by Morganprint Blackheath Ltd

British Library Cataloguing in Publication Data

Cameron, Norman, *1905–1953*
    Collected poems and selected translations.
    I. Title   II. Hope, Warren, *1944–*   III. Barker,
    Jonathan, *1949–*
    821'.912

    ISBN 0 85646 202 0

Contents

II *Later poems from* WORK IN HAND,
    FORGIVE ME, SIRE *and uncollected poems*

III Juvenilia

IV Selections from FRANÇOIS VILLON

V Other Translations

Introduction

This is the first complete edition of Norman Cameron's poems to appear in Britain. It includes thirteen previously uncollected poems and translations found by Warren Hope and included in his important 1985 American edition of *The Complete Poems of Norman Cameron*. The present book, with its new critical introduction and biographical essay, is the product of the shared transatlantic enthusiasm of Warren Hope and myself for the work of a poet whom we both see as unjustly neglected. It is puzzling why Cameron's moving and quietly memorable poems are not more widely appreciated by critics – they are surely some of the most elegant, intelligent and enjoyable poems of the thirties and forties. But where literary critics have in the main failed to recognize the worth of the poems, Cameron's fellow poets such as Roy Fuller, Robert Graves, Geoffrey Grigson and James Reeves have spoken up for them. And recently a later generation of poets, including John Fuller, Francis Hope, Mick Imlah and Peter Porter have found their way to them too; possibly, like me, led there by the issue of Ian Hamilton's magazine *The Review* (Nos. 27–28 for Autumn–Winter 1971–72) which included a symposium of new essays on Cameron.

In his lifetime Norman Cameron published just three short books of poems: *The Winter House and Other Poems*, Dent, 1935; *Work in Hand* (with Alan Hodge and Robert Graves), published 'under a single cover for economy and friendship', The Hogarth Press, 1942; and *Forgive Me, Sire*, Fore Publications, 1950. Prior to book publication poems appeared in the annual *Oxford Poetry* anthologies for 1925 to 1928, and in literary periodicals such as Geoffrey Grigson's *New Verse* in the thirties and Cyril Connolly's *Horizon* in the forties. Cameron also published verse translations from a number of poets, but especially Arthur Rimbaud (an edition of all his translations from Rimbaud is also published by Anvil); and François Villon (a selection from the Villon translations is included here in section four).

Cameron was commissioned to translate the prose of French authors such as Baudelaire, Voltaire and Balzac, but as he pointed out in the questionnaire quoted in full on page 142, 'I write a poem because I think it wants to be written'.[1] After Cameron's death in April 1953 at the age of 48 Alan Hodge compiled *The Collected Poems of Norman Cameron 1905–1953*, published by The Hogarth Press in 1957, and containing a total of fifty-nine poems, some previously uncollected. Also included was an introduction by Robert Graves, which commented that 'Though I never made a deliberate attempt to memorize Norman's work, a good half of it has become firmly fixed in my head, and I could not quote more than two or three lines of his ambitious contemporaries.' Graves also noted that Cameron 'wrote as he talked, unrhetorically, with careful thought for the clarity of his phrases, and frequent recourse to the *Oxford English Dictionary* in search of a decent precedent for every unusual word. His rhymes were exact; and he seems to have taken technique for granted, never feeling the need either for imitation or experiment.'

A similar point was made by Geoffrey Grigson in a review of *The Winter House*, where he sees Cameron as 'not a moral poet ... not interested in uplift, and he is not, at any distance from immediate politics, a politician ... he is not a professional poet, writing his twenty lines a day, he is not a literary chap ... he is a natural poet, with all the virtue, and all the limitations, of the spontaneous amateur. His poems are not forced ... They are each an expanded image, an event, with the organic or circular nature of an event.' Grigson concludes 'That is to say, they are a genuine pure poetry ... One need only enjoy them without wishing that they were bigger or better, as one enjoys nursery rhymes or folk song.'[2]

Kenneth Allott, another contemporary of Cameron, also saw him as a natural poet: 'Edwin Muir has described Cameron as "a neat, semi-epigrammatic poet", but this is a tepid way of referring to his precision and skill with words. *The Winter House* is a collection in which no single poem appears to have

[1] *New Verse*, No. 11, October 1934.

[2] *New Verse*, No. 19, February–March 1936; review of *The Winter House and Other Poems*.

been forced. His poems wear well, and I suspect that they may be read when some fancied modern poets with much bigger reputations are quite forgotten.'[3] This is true, but in fact Muir's description is fair enough. In 'Forgive Me, Sire', a poem written for Robert Graves, Cameron referred to himself as 'One of the neat ones in your awkward squad', and his poems *do* have a concise 'semi-epigrammatic' appearance.

In an essay on Cameron Roy Fuller comments on the 'clarity, shapeliness and neutrality' of the poems, and also expresses the interesting theory that 'Cameron fathered a whole mass of brief mythologic-anecdotal poetry in the thirties, so characteristic of the time but now perhaps not thought to be one of its main features. Cameron's verse was an antidote to the rhetoric of the left and to the imitations of Auden, and so helped several poets who would otherwise have wholly succumbed to those diseases to turn out a few decent poems.'[4] I am sure this could be as true of Cameron's example during the forties. By remaining just outside the mainstream of both decades, Cameron's own work appears today less damaged by changes in literary styles than that of some of his contemporaries.

Elsewhere Roy Fuller pointed out that Cameron's 'clever style changed remarkably little from the interesting poems he published in the school magazine at Fettes under the *nom de plume* "Billiken".'[5] This is an important point also made by Martin Seymour-Smith, who wrote that Cameron 'resembled Graves and was a close friend of his and of Laura Riding's – but he was not substantially influenced by either; this can be demonstrated but is seldom believed. He formed his style while still at Oxford, as the sequence of poems included by Auden in *Oxford Poetry 1927* shows.'[6] We do not know if the teenage poet who published the distinctly un-Gravesian 'Disease of the Mind', 'The Death-Bed of P. Aelius Hadrianus

[3] *The Penguin Book of Contemporary Verse*, Penguin, 1950.

[4] *The Review*, Nos. 27–28, Autumn–Winter 1971–72; containing a symposium of essays on Cameron by Francis Hope, Geoffrey Grigson, James Reeves, Roy Fuller and G. S. Fraser.

[5] *London Magazine*, August–September, 1985; review of *The Complete Poems of Norman Cameron* edited and introduced by Warren Hope.

[6] *Guide to Modern World Literature*, third edition, Macmillan, 1985.

Imperator' and 'A Song' (all included here for the first time) in *The Fettesian* school magazine for 1923 and 1924 had already read the first books of Robert Graves. It would have been difficult – although not impossible – for Cameron to have found his way to Graves's poems much before the widely available *Augustan Books of Modern Poetry* series edition of 1925 or the *Poems 1914–1926* published in 1927, the year that Graves himself said the two first met.[7] Yet a reading of Graves's *Poems 1914–1926*, his first of many volumes of collected poems, tends to support rather than refute the argument that Cameron was not substantially influenced by Graves. Cameron concentrates always on a narrow and extremely consistent stylistic range with great success, and has none of Graves's fiery lyric attack; nor does he command the sheer variety of kinds of poem – from dramatic lyrics and narratives, to Skeltonics, ballads or modern nursery rhymes – of which the older poet was master. The two certainly became friends and may well have learnt from each other's work, but it is evident that the relationship was far nearer that of equals with shared poetic affinities and a similar sense of what poetry was and was not, than the master / student rôle which tends to be assumed.

The poems of Cameron and Graves certainly have much more *stylistically* in common with the rhythmic directness of the native English tradition of Thomas Hardy, A. E. Housman, Edward Thomas or Rudyard Kipling than with either the first poems of W. H. Auden, C. Day Lewis and Louis Mac-Neice, or the work of the modernists F. S. Flint, T. S. Eliot and Ezra Pound. And yet these differences apart, both Cameron and Graves share with both groups of poets an ability to express the complex and puzzled consciousness of modern man, as in Cameron's early 'Dwellers in the Sea':

> My soul is some leviathan in vague distress
> That travels up great slopes of hills beneath the sea.
> > Up from the darkness and the heaviness
> > Into a slowly gathering radiancy.

---

[7] *The Collected Poems of Norman Cameron 1905–1953*, The Hogarth Press, 1957; with an introduction by Robert Graves.

Juvenilia maybe, but in its way as impressive as Geoffrey Hill's early poem 'Genesis' and showing a similar marked affinity with the poet's later work. Both Graves and Cameron shared a grounding in the work of the classical authors, as is evident in Cameron's 'Nunc Scio Quid Sit Amor' with its three-line Latin epigraph from Virgil's Eighth Eclogue. This taste probably contributed to the rather formal and restrained style of Cameron's poems, one thing noticeably setting them apart from the work of his Oxford contemporaries; although a total of six of Cameron's poems were included by Auden and Day Lewis in *Oxford Poetry 1927*, along with poems by themselves, Louis MacNeice, Clere Parsons, Rex Warner and others.[8] The link with Auden was a long one: as well as appearing in a number of the *Oxford Poetry* anthologies with W. H. Auden, Cameron also appeared as J. N. Cameron with a certain W. H. Arden (the latter clearly a misprint, the former, the form of his name under which Cameron's early poems appeared) in *Public School Verse: An Anthology 1923–24* published in 1924.

Support for the argument that Cameron was not stylistically influenced by Graves comes too from the poet James Reeves, who in a review of the 1957 *Collected Poems* wrote: 'Half the poems in this book appeared as *The Winter House* in 1935. Most of these would pass for contemporary in the magazines of today. Cameron's style, which he seems to have all but perfected as an undergraduate in the twenties, has been silently adopted by a generation of younger poets.'[9] Reeves refers here to the fifties generation of Movement poets who came to prominence in George Hartley's magazine *Listen* and Robert Conquest's *New Lines* anthology, and whose number included Kingsley Amis, Donald Davie, John Holloway, Elizabeth Jennings, Philip Larkin and John Wain.

This view is also taken by Martin Seymour-Smith who noted that Cameron 'wrote a witty and metaphysical poetry – frequently laced with deep feeling – that foreshadowed the

---

[8] 'Pretty Maids all in a Row', 'The Thespians at Thermopylae', 'Decapitation of Is', 'Virgin Russia', 'Marine Lament', 'Rhinegold'; the last appeared in a variant form as 'The Diver'.

[9] Reprinted in *Essays: Commitment to Poetry*, Heinemann, 1969.

style of the so-called Movement of the fifties.'[10] Seymour-Smith's comment on the 'witty and metaphysical poetry' of Cameron puts us in mind of the thirties poet William Empson, renowned for intellectual argufying in graceful stanzas. Empson, like Cameron, wrote little: his first book was published in 1935, the same year as *The Winter House*, but his second and final book of poems *The Gathering Storm* appeared in 1940, a decade before Cameron's *Forgive Me, Sire*. Empson is the more intellectually robust of the two, but there are similarities; both employ irony, wit, extended metaphor and at times fantastic imagery, and force the reader to work at their poems before the mix of thought and feeling becomes clear. In fact the combined influence of the subtly experimental yet traditional poetries of Norman Cameron, William Empson, Roy Fuller and Robert Graves surely contributed hugely to the poetry of the Movement era, which returned to traditional forms with a new vigour and purpose after the predominantly rhetorical style of the forties.

Cameron's own lack of rhetorical flourish was remarked on by the poet Francis Hope who wrote: 'An almost impenetrable discretion surrounds both life and letters. His friends sometimes called him "Normal Cameron" and one of them apparently exclaimed: "How one envies Norman's life! No detail at all!"'[11] The friend who coined the 'Normal Cameron' tag was Dylan Thomas about whom Cameron wrote the affectionately critical 'The Dirty Little Accuser'. Stylistically Francis Hope's idea of the 'impenetrable discretion' of the poems is linked to Roy Fuller's comment on their 'clarity, shapeliness and neutrality' which makes the personality of the poet secondary to the formal needs of the poem. Paradoxically, as I have already stated, a close examination of the poems reveals that, beneath this surface restraint, there lies a complicated and perplexed modern sensibility. Cameron shares with Philip Larkin, the most significant post-war British poet, the ability to express through an apparently diffident persona, a personal and metaphysical frustration on behalf of his readers. His poems are formal constructions – neutral surfaces if you like – in which

---

[10] *Guide to Modern World Literature*, third edition, Macmillan, 1985.

[11] *The Review*, Nos. 27–28, Autumn–Winter 1971–72.

the form is carefully, even meticulously controlled, but where the feeling is often, in the words of Martin Seymour-Smith, that of a 'fiercely romantic nature'.[12] This is certainly the case of those poems in *The Winter House* which employ extended metaphor, fantastic imagery and a direct yet, at times, tortuous diction.

Geoffrey Grigson drew attention to Cameron's 'individual imaginative products of introversion, a good many (e.g. "Public-House Confidence", "Mountain Monastery", "The Unfinished Race", "The Disused Temple", "By Leave of Luck") body out phantasies which are the community's as well as Mr Cameron's.'[13] This is a subtle point, which I will return to later, but there are other of Cameron's allegories which it is doubtful if many of 'the community' would share; such as the phantasmagoric battle between a traveller and the challenged 'jeering water-ghost' of 'Fight with a Water-Spirit'. The contest between man and spirit is of course impossible, and eventually the spirit reappears in the water, leaving the traveller to accept defeat:

> No use to fight.
> Better to give the place a holy name,
> Go on with less ambition than I came.

That acceptance of both ridiculousness and what W. H. Auden called 'human unsuccess', is to be found in other poems of spiritual questioning, such as 'The Successor', 'The Disused Temple', and 'No Remedy' on the nature of evil:

> Set a priest against a witch:
> They mirror until who knows which?
> Boast you have cut out evil, but
> What is the outline round the cut?

'Moonlight, Waterlight and Opal' turns these unanswerable questions into a positive acceptance of 'nothingness', somehow learnt from the 'glitter, like a mirror's face' of the unearthly trio of the title:

---

[12] *Who's Who in Modern World Literature*, Weidenfeld & Nicolson, 1976.

[13] *New Verse*, No. 19, February–March 1936; review of *The Winter House and Other Poems*.

> These moonbeam niceties, sweet to undergo,
> Have been an austere discipline, the less
> Exceptionable in that trifling so
> I've learned to be content with nothingness.

Cameron's love poems show a similar interest in 'nothing-
ness' and a willing acceptance of a lack of success which is
nonetheless never total failure, as in 'From a Woman to a
Greedy Lover' quoted entire:

> What is this recompense you'd have from me?
> Melville asked no compassion of the sea.
> Roll to and fro, forgotten in my wrack,
> Love as you please – I owe you nothing back.

Or the disruptive 'fierce outlander who has swooped' on the
individual in 'Nunc Scio Quid Sit Amor':

> And from his savage smell I can't go free.
> I fear you and I fear you, barbarous Love.
> You are no citizen of my country.

There is 'the hot, aching man of blood within' of 'Let Him
Loose', the 'Blood beating in my head sang me towards ruin'
of 'The Downward Pulse', and the 'ruinous working of that
inward heat/That I had hoped would serve to warm my bed'
which melts the 'showering snow' of self-restraint needed to
fight the unruly emotions in 'The Winter House'. Interestingly,
the emotional coolness and order which prove so desirable yet
elusive, are clearly present in the quiet artistry which fashions
disarray into formal order in these poems.

But the victory of the human spirit over adversity is a real
presence in the work too. There is something wholehearted
about Cameron's acceptance of difficulty which makes the
poems liberating rather than low-key or depressing. In the
allegory 'A Visit to the Dead' a traveller buys a passage to a
living death in the 'small and pent' 'regions of the dead', but is
saved by a dawning sense of the ridiculousness of their closed
and petty world:

Long I was caught up in their twilit strife.
Almost they got me, almost had me weaned
From all my memory of life.
But laughter supervened:

Laughter, like sunlight in the cucumber,
The innermost resource, that does not fail.
I, Marco Polo, traveller,
Am back, with what a tale!

As we have seen, the traveller theme appears in many of Cameron's mature tale poems. It dates back to the early meditation on life after death, 'Dwellers in the Sea':

We have but rumours, unsubstantial tales;
And who would give his life up for a story?

But there is another side to Cameron – one looking outside onto a world of specific things and events. Chief among these poems are those coming out of Cameron's experiences in World War II where he appears at last free from introspection, as in 'Black Takes White' or 'Green, Green is El Aghir':

Green, green is El Aghir. It has a railway-station,
And the wealth of its soil has borne many another fruit,
A mairie, a school and an elegant Salle de Fêtes.
Such blessings, as I remarked, in effect, to the waiter,
Are added unto them that have plenty of water.

The larger ironies continue to dominate here but there is a more relaxed and personal feel present too, as in 'Wörther See' on soldiers at play away from combat: 'Would that wars might end for all soldiers like this' the poem begins and ends. Another poem, 'The Invader', presents the invader, despite evident victory, as frustrated through finding himself 'At once the oppressor and the slave'. We are again reminded of Philip Larkin, this time through the sense of 'fulfilment's desolate attic' present in Larkin's poem 'Deceptions' written in 1950 and included in *The Less Deceived*.

This more objective, almost journalistic, side to Cameron's work returns us to Grigson's comment quoted earlier on those poems which 'body out phantasies which are the community's as well as Mr Cameron's'.[14] These poems are concise moral tales able to buttonhole the reader in the manner of biblical parables. Norman Cameron may seem at first sight an unlikely maker of modern myths, but that is what tales such as 'The Firm of Happiness, Limited', 'A Hook for Leviathan', 'The Unfinished Race' and 'Public-House Confidence' are nearest to. The last mentioned is spoken by one who manages to be paid as both a manual and office worker while in fact, as he confesses: 'I am no use at all to either, / And draw the pay of both for doing neither.' In Cameron's personal mythology he is a lone, if dishonest victor over circumstance. 'A Hook for Leviathan' returns to the early Leviathan theme and tells the story of the tons of steel needed to forge both line and massive hook in an absurd attempt to catch the mythical sea monster:

> And if you ask: 'Where will you find the vessel
> To carry such a hook?' the owners stare:
> 'Surely we have enough with which to wrestle.
> We're not ship-builders. That's not out affair.'

Mick Imlah has referred to these poems as 'cool fantasies', and the description is a good one. No matter how near to satire the poems get, Cameron is always too far from the cutting edge of true satire and too near the essentially accepting spirit of comedy for him to want to do more than observe and accept the situation as inevitable. 'The Firm of Happiness, Limited' is one of his most successful poems of human unhappiness and failure. The 'firm' goes bust, but is then purchased on a mortgage in a reckless 'mingled impulse of thrift and pity'. But the 'Laughter, like sunlight in the cucumber' of 'A Visit to the Dead' has gone:

> Now nobody knows what to do with this monstrous hulk
>   we have bought.
> At the last Corporation meeting one alderman, half in jest,
> Spoke of turning it into a barracks. Meanwhile there's
>   the dreary thought
> That we ratepayers have to keep paying the burdensome
>   interest.

---

[14] *New Verse*, No. 19, February–March 1936; review of *The Winter House and Other Poems*.

All of Cameron's poems have in common a formal elegance and an ironic detached tone, qualities which eventually serve to make him a strangely elusive poetic personality. But the voice is unmistakeably his own and engaging too, no matter how uningratiating and impersonal his poems might at first sight appear. In the end, despite all their major differences of ambition, output and range, Cameron shares a need for traditional forms, not just with Robert Graves, but perhaps less obviously with his contemporary W. H. Auden, who shortly before his death commented that: 'On hedonistic grounds, I am a fanatical formalist. To me, a poem is, among other things, always a verbal game.'[15] The 'fanatical formalist' side of Cameron agreed with Auden, just as another side of him provided the emotional depths which the formalist then shaped. For Cameron the vital frame of form was necessary before he could truly be himself as a poet of feeling.

JONATHAN BARKER

---

[15] *Agenda* special issue on rhythm, Vol. 10 No. 4–Vol. 11 No. 1, Autumn–Winter 1972–73.

A Note on this Edition

This edition is based on Warren Hope's 1985 American edition of the poems, published by R. L. Barth, which did not include the translations. The text and punctuation is that of *The Collected Poems of Norman Cameron 1905–1953* published by The Hogarth Press in 1957, and prepared for the press by Cameron's friend and literary executor Alan Hodge, who with the help of Cameron's widow, Gretl, incorporated the author's final preferences into the edition. The few significant departures from the texts of the three books published during Cameron's lifetime are given on pages 153–4, but no variants from earlier versions of the poems are included. The thirteen previously uncollected poems and the translations of Heine and Nezval were all discovered during the course of research by Warren Hope.

The order of the poems in section one follows that of *The Winter House and Other Poems* (the only book of his in which Cameron appears to have had a guiding hand in deciding the order); with three additional poems originally printed in *Oxford Poetry* for 1927 and 1928 inserted chronologically. Section two includes all Cameron's later poems, including those published in *Work in Hand*, the majority of which appeared later, with additional poems, in *Forgive Me, Sire*. The order of poems both here and in section three of juvenilia is based on Warren Hope's researches into the order of composition and, where applicable, first publication. Section four consists of a selection of Cameron's translations from Villon's fifteenth-century French into seventeenth-century English while maintaining the original verse-forms. Section five represents three other translations. A separate edition of Cameron's complete translations from Rimbaud is also published by Anvil.

WARREN HOPE
JONATHAN BARKER

London, June 1988

I

The Winter House and Other Poems

and poems from

Oxford Poetry

NUNC SCIO QUID SIT AMOR

Nunc scio quid sit Amor: duris in cotibus illum
Aut Tmaros aut Rhodope, aut extremi Garamantes,
Nec generis nostri puerum nec sanguinis edunt.

   (Virgil's Eighth Eclogue)

From lands where all the flowers have teeth, where half
A serpent-furlong coils round every tree,
Where the wild rainbow like a great giraffe
Curves down its neck to drink upon the sea,
Has come this most outrageous foreigner,
This fierce outlander who has swooped on me,
And like a peacock's tail keeps hanging there
Above my shoulder, where I turn and see
Tall flames – or are they pinions? – stream above.
And from his savage smell I can't go free.
I fear you and I fear you, barbarous Love.
You are no citizen of my country.

PRETTY MAIDS ALL IN A ROW

(From a hand-book of advice to travellers)

And in those glades
Where Mary keeps,
Growing waist-deep,
Her pretty maids,
Make no rude haste
Too soon to know
How they may grow
Below the waist.
Or you will find
At the first wrench
No lovely wench,
But rough green rind.
The tender fruit
Down in the mould
Ends in a cold
And gritty root.

THE THESPIANS AT THERMOPYLAE

The honours that the people give always
Pass to those use-besotted gentlemen
Whose numskull courage is a kind of fear,
A fear of thought and of the oafish mothers
('Or with your shield or on it') in their rear.
Spartans cannot retreat. Why, then, their praise
For going forward should be less than others'.
But we, actors and critics of one play,
Of sober-witted judgment, who could see
So many roads, and chose the Spartan way,
What has the popular report to say
Of us, the Thespians at Thermopylae?

DECAPITATION OF IS

We tried one day to execute old Is.
For his predicative, Protean vis-
Age had so much disturbed our peace of mind.
But though it needed no long time to find
The axe of reason and the block of fact,
All ready for that sanitary act,
We were prevented by one curious check:
None knew exactly where to find his neck.
'The deed is most humane; Is never feels.
Strike here,' said one, and pointed at his heels.
'Strike there,' said two; but what he meant by there,
His pointing finger proved, was old Is' hair.
Meanwhile Is' face was working horribly,
Until a sudden fear made us agree
To give the business up. In any case
We had not aimed to turn him into Was.

VIRGIN RUSSIA

In search of Eldorados in the snow
Or subtler fury, who can know?
From many quarters have my armies gone
(Darius, Charles of Sweden, Bonaparte)
Marching on virgin Russia. And each one
Has met defeat by the same simple art
Of burning towns before and not behind.
The only impress made on that virgin
Is of dead armies stretching like long scars,
With snow for healing overskin.

What is the cost of these vain wars?
The armies killed not so much loss I find.
Armies are built again
With ease, for this campaign.
But my rich cornlands, that once lined
The Russian border, broken by the tread
Of my own forces, gathering for the raid.

MARINE LAMENT

Queen Thetis' darlings, weep, you halcyons!
Halcyons, weep! Let every beast that swims
Or wears the sea-god's lovely livery
Grieve for the lord of these dominions.
Glaucus laments his beauty gone, his limbs
Blurred into dreary wreckage by the sea.
The penguins stand aghast to hear the moan
Of Glaucus floating sadly in the bay,
An old, old man, crabs tangled in his hair,
With shells and sucking creatures overgrown,
Sea-lichenous hands all webbed and worn away.
Trailing long fans of sea-weed watch him float
Like an old fragment of a broken boat.

FIGHT WITH A WATER-SPIRIT

Though many men had passed the ford, not one
Had ever seen that jeering water-ghost
Denying their true conquest of the stream.
But I, who saw him smile behind a stone,
Stopped, challenged him to justify his boast.
Then came the fight, exhausting as a dream,
With stuff not quite impalpable. He sank,
Sighing, at last, in a small shrinking pile.
But my victorious paean changed to fright
To see once more the pale curve of his flank
There in the water, and his endless smile
Broaden behind the stone. No use to fight.
Better to give the place a holy name,
Go on with less ambition than I came.

RHINEGOLD

. . . refracted angles shine;
Not all the Rhinegold in the Rhine
Could tempt me further downwards. Dazed
By weight of water, almost crazed
By tilted and perplexing planes
I seek the surface. Now remains
No sign but water-flattened hair
I was so near the Rhinegold there,
Fool, agued fool! While those glib cheats
Peddle their gold-bricks in the streets.

CENTRAL EUROPE

Despite their boastful Margraves and their flags
The inland years – fat peasants winterbound,
Stunned by the heat of their enormous stoves,
Whimpering fear of baleful gods and wolves –
Have set a bloody darkness in their souls.
Still they can see, fixed amid this red haze
Of swimming particles, the forest-faces,
Come, following the deeper shade, to town.

They need a wind bringing up gulls and salt,
Sailors and nabobs with new foreign gifts,
To blow their crannies free of ancient fear.

THE VOYAGE TO SECRECY

The morn of his departure, men could say
'Either by such a way or such a way,'
And, a week later, still, by plotting out
The course of all the roadways round about,
'In these some score of places he may be.'
How many days the voyage to secrecy?
Always the milestones by the road hark back
To whence he came, and those in idleness
Can bound his range with map and compasses.

When shall their compasses strain wide and crack,
And alien milestones, with strange figures,
Baffle the sagest of geographers?

THE BEASTS OF CIRCUMSTANCE

We are the favoured beasts
Of Circumstance's company.
Close by the table where he feasts
We purr and praise and pray
Beneath his hand all day.
Now, though we have not heard the shout
Of enemies who storm without,
We suddenly cringe askance,
No longer at his beck,
To feel the hand of Circumstance
Turn blind and witless on the neck.

THE SECOND AUTUMN

After our damsons and coarse harvesting
Follows the second autumn, for that brood
Whose unseen revel sets us hankering.
They get fine pasture in the bonfire smoke
And idle moistures spilled for no man's food.
Anguished by feasting-smells fit to provoke
A hunger that there's no appeasing, stand
The human masters outcast on their land.

Then plunge your teeth stone-deep in the known fruit
Lest the deceiving odours work on you
And lead you out to dabble like a brute
Naked in the unwholesome dusk and dew.

THE WINTER HOUSE

Out of the showering snow itself to build
Under the lintel that the eyebrows form
A winter house, whose phantom planks are filled
By old storm holding back against new storm,
By flakes too numerous for enmity
(No room to hate a multitude); and so
To shelter under a false canopy
And play at happy hutman in the snow
– This cannot last for long; a prickly threat
Assails me, of disaster overhead,
The ruinous working of that inward heat
That I had hoped would serve to warm my bed.
Now may the coward eyebrows try in vain
To re-assert the downward-pouring roof.
It honourably joins the snow again,
And comes to put my native fire to proof.

PUBLIC-HOUSE CONFIDENCE

Well, since you're from the other side of town,
I'll tell you how I hold a soft job down.
In the designing-rooms and laboratory
I'm dressed in overalls, and so pretend
To be on business from the factory.
The workmen think I'm from the other end.
The in-betweens and smart commission-men
Believe I must have some pull with the boss.
So, playing off the spanner against the pen,
I never let the rumour get across
Of how I am no use at all to either,
And draw the pay of both for doing neither.

NO REMEDY

Smite the devil underground:
It blooms with danger all around.
Or set a stone and write on it
Hic Antichristus obiit.
The verb is nothing, but the name
Remains triumphant and the same.
Set a priest against a witch:
They mirror until who knows which?
Boast you have cut out evil, but
What is the outline round the cut?
What hieroglyph remains to teach
You letters of unholy speech?
Smite and declaim and cut away,
There he was and there he'll stay.

COMICAL MEN

Comical men, you can imagine them
With heads alone, served up like John the Baptist,
Set solid on the platter, with a droll
Squareheadedness, like boulders on the ground,
Or like a heavy clown's head in a ruff,
A lubber schoolboy peeping over a desk.
The body's never there; the face's pucker
Twists it away behind. We interpose
A pedestal to hide the shrimpish coil.

RELEASE FROM FEVER

Lying in fever, while tornado-weather
Strained up to body-heat and storm sky high,
I waged a wordy struggle, in shame and anger,
With flimsy devils hanging from the air.
My fever and the storm both broke together,
And rain and sweat descended. There was I
From flowery strains and stresses a seed dropped,
Released from long, hysterical argument
Of which the tornado-thunder's first explosion
Was the last frantic gesture and good-bye.
Then, as I lay on soaking earth,
There came what stomach-filling mirth
And low, strong exultation!

FOR THE FLY-LEAF OF A SCHOOL-BOOK

One of the more intelligent members
Of the upper-middle classes
Of the most important country
On the nearest-but-two planet to the sun,
I send my prayer unto Thee.

Now reverse this address,
And carry it further
With sections and quarterings
And split the last atom
And come unto Me.

THE SUCCESSOR

My spark flew round and round the outer ring,
Challenged the flame of his burnt-offering,
That knew the menace, and went small and blue.
And old Sadokiel wavered, and the dark
Ushered him outward, through the small priests' door.
And all the people shouted, and my spark
Descended on the altar with a roar
Of rising flame. And I stood forth, the new
High Priest, when lo there, lo! how the flame threw
A well-known antique shadow on the floor,
The tall cap and the beard just as before
– I was Sadokiel! And now menacing
A spark flew round and round the outer ring.

ALL THINGS ILL DONE

All things ill done, and quitted hopefully
As islands no more visited – the sea
That washes round that archipelago
Must somewhere have another shore. And so
Confronted by a sinister stagnation
I recognize in it my own creation.
Sea, time, old binding-link of separation
That I had left, a fain-forgotten shift,
Has coiled around, offering its blank gift.

RIMBAUD AND VERLAINE

The commerce between Rimbaud and Verlaine –
As when two hostile peoples, mountain and plain,
Appoint a special place for bartering,
Where one by day and one by night, they bring
Their wares, their own mere superfluity –
It was too easily won, this decency,
And readily had a dismal end, because
They did not keep their hours; and so it was
That overlapped and meeting in twilight
These two hated each other at half-sight.

MOUNTAIN MONASTERY

The monks came here at length as colonists
For the spent empire of the centuries,
And set stone walls by rocks that owed allegiance
Separately, outside the centuries.

But what unease comes of this spatial trick,
This hard-as-a-stone but senseless juxtaposition.
For mountain or monastery, either or both,
Must seem, when viewed askance from the other's position,

Obdurate though dislodged, as the teeth in fever
Become uncouth in the head, like chapels or rocks,
The elements of a nightmare of stone edges,
A jarring of monks and teeth and monkish rocks.

LET HIM LOOSE

Should the hot, aching man of blood within
Ever attain the surface as he wishes,
Flushing his veins up over all the skin,
Net of splenetically throbbing meshes –

Why, then, I'm hot on the hot world, indeed.
The inner and the outer conflagration
Are spilled together, and one giddy creed
Spins off with the last wisp of demarcation.

But this is false: for he is not my foe;
He struggles only to rejoin his kind.
But let him loose a moment, see him go
Into a cloud or travelling down some wind.

SUMMER'S SLAVE

What have you now to answer, summer's slave,
To autumn's cold call of emancipation,
What, beside gooseflesh? Indeed, summer's slave
Can never be the citizen of winter.
It would be wiser, then, to keep your livery.
Follow your master in his sulky exile
Off to some feudal, decorative coast;
An easy life, obtaining sustenance
From gossip and report of winter's doings,
Knowing the body politic of winter
Is well established without help from you.

A CALENDAR-FLUSH

The calendar tells him of so-many journeys;
Also, in confirmation, he remembers
Passing by numerous tolls and fords and bridges,
The tolls – they led through half a dozen lands;
He'd been well stocked, it seemed, with foreign moneys.
The fords – he must have had long legs for them.
The bridges – how many thousand riveters
Did they recall? Distracted now he seeks
To fit these numerous tolls and fords and bridges
In a continuous road, to reassemble
Income, boot-leather and the building-trade;
And draws and draws for necessary cards
To fill a calendar-flush of travelling days.

THE UNFINISHED RACE

No runner clears the final fence,
The laurels have long since gone stale.
They must be a cardboard pretence,
These watchers crowded on the rail.

For why should crowds stay watching so
To see a race that has no end?
How many centuries ago
The runners came up round the bend.

Always they balk at this last leap,
And then recoil to try once more.
From pride or custom still they keep
On striving – those once at the fore

Distinguished only from the ruck
By their impressive long run back.

SHE AND I

She and I, we thought and fought
And each of us won by the other's defeat;
She and I, we danced and pranced
And lost by neglect the use of our feet;
She and I caught ills and chills
And were cured or dead before we could cough;
She and I, we walked and talked
Half an hour after our heads were cut off.

IT'S A FINE THING

It's a fine thing to be a rhymer – glee
It is to let your lust and spite run rife,
But so disguised that should the master threaten
'Sirrah, the whip!' the fool can prance and simper
'Whoop Jug, I love thee! Nothing but a story.
It happened in Queen Anne's reign, and she's dead.
All's fair in rhyming.' Fool, I loathe your fancies.
Whether they flit, in search of sanctuary,
To Queen Anne's reign or to Cloudcuckooland,
Dodging the whip, the faggot and the axe,
They ring too sharp an echo from here and now.

THE DISUSED TEMPLE

When once the scourging prophet, with his cry
Of 'money-changers' and 'my Father's house,'
Had set his mark upon it, men were shy
To enter, and the fane fell in disuse.

Since it was unfrequented and left out
Of living, what was there to do except
Make fast the door, destroy the key? (No doubt
One of our number did it while we slept.)

It stays as a disquieting encumbrance.
We moved the market-place out of its shade;
But still it overhangs our whole remembrance,
Making us both inquisitive and afraid.

Shrewd acousticians hammer on the door
And study from the echoes what is there;
Meaningless yet familiar, these appear
Much what we would expect – but we're not sure.

Disquiet makes us sleepy; shoddiness
Has come upon our crafts. No question that
We'll shortly have to yield to our distress,
Abandon the whole township, and migrate.

MEETING MY FORMER SELF

Meeting my former self in a nostalgia
Of confident, confiding recognition,
Offering him an island in the Atlantic –
Half-way, I said, from Tenerife to England.
Great cliffs of chalk slope from the fishing-village
Up to the lighthouse. Rum sold free of duty.
Only the fishermen and lighthouse-keeper
Besides ourselves. Drinking the rum, card-playing
And walking in the wastes of stone and cactus
And meeting the mail-steamer once a fortnight.
– But these inducements pitifully withered
At his embarrassed look. Turning to welcome
A friend he had acquired since our last meeting,
Not known to me, he spoke of other matters;
And I was weeping and humiliated.

BY LEAVE OF LUCK

Once through the gate, the horns and light,
The feast and honorific song
So cheered us that it was not long
Before we took them as of right,

Not thinking how we'd merited,
But, giving thanks to luck, forgot
The land of hardship we had fled
Where luck was no part of man's lot.

But this complacence was cut short;
Their flattering jubilation died
As though it needed a new guide;
A spokesman stood out from our court.

'Sirs, we have feasted; now relieve
This waiting, and announce the end
For which you came.' 'Simply, good friend,
To join your feast.' 'And by whose leave?'

'By leave of luck.' 'Should luck, indeed,
Prompt these vast honours to a stranger?
We had supposed you came to read
Some riddle, or dispel a danger.'

'Simply as common men we came.'
'How dared you, by the heroes' gate?'
'We purposed no heroic claim.'
'But you disown it now too late.'

THE COMPASSIONATE FOOL

My enemy had bidden me as guest.
His table all set out with wine and cake,
His ordered chairs, he to beguile me dressed
So neatly, moved my pity for his sake.

I knew it was an ambush, but could not
Leave him to eat his cake up by himself
And put his unused glasses on the shelf.
I made pretence of falling in his plot,

And trembled when in his anxiety
He bared it too absurdly to my view.
And even as he stabbed me through and through
I pitied him for his small strategy.

NAKED AMONG THE TREES

Formerly he had been a well-loved god,
Each visit from him a sweet episode,
Not like the outrageous Pentecostal rush
Or wilful Jahveh shrieking from a bush.

He bloomed in our bodies to the finger-tips
And rose like barley-sugar round the lips,
Then unawares was cleanly gone away,
With no relapse or aftertaint to pay.

We've forced the burgeoned lust he gave to us
Into a thousand manners of misuse,
Into the hot alarms, wishes and frets,
The drinking-bouts, the boasting and the bets.

And these have made his cult degenerate,
So that the booted Puritan magistrate
Did right to spur down on the devotees,
Catch them and whip them naked among the trees.

II

Later poems from
Work in Hand
Forgive Me, Sire
and uncollected poems

FORGIVE ME, SIRE

Forgive me, Sire, for cheating your intent,
That I, who should command a regiment,
Do amble amiably here, O God,
One of the neat ones in your awkward squad.

NOSTALGIA FOR DEATH

Psychologists discovered that Miss B
Suffered from a split personality.
She had B-1, B-2, 3, 4 and 5,
All of them struggling in one body alive.
B-1 got tipsy and B-2 felt ill,
B-3 got pregnant, B-4 paid the bill.
Well, that's enough of that. What about me?
I have, at least, N-1, N-2, N-3.
N-1 is a glutton, N-2 is a miser,
N-3 is different, but not much wiser.
Well, that's enough of that. What of N-O?
That is the N I'd really like to know.

THREE LOVE POEMS

FROM A WOMAN TO A GREEDY LOVER

What is this recompense you'd have from me?
Melville asked no compassion of the sea.
Roll to and fro, forgotten in my wrack,
Love as you please – I owe you nothing back.

IN THE QUEEN'S ROOM

In smoky outhouses of the court of love
I chattered, a recalcitrant underling
Living on scraps. 'Below stairs or above,
All's one,' I said. 'We valets have our fling.'

Now I am come, by a chance beyond reach,
Into your room, my body smoky and soiled
And on my tongue the taint of chattering speech,
Tell me, Queen, am I irredeemably spoiled?

SHEPHERDESS

All day my sheep have mingled with yours. They strayed
Into your valley seeking a change of ground.
Held and bemused with what they and I had found,
Pastures and wonders, heedlessly I delayed.

Now it is late. The tracks leading home are steep,
The stars and landmarks in your country are strange.
How can I take my sheep back over the range?
Shepherdess, show me now where I may sleep.

MOONLIGHT, WATERLIGHT AND OPAL

'Moonlight, Waterlight and Opal are good
Corinthians, bad friends for a young man,'
Said I, cronelike in my self-motherhood –
Jealous, perhaps, for the more homely clan.

I loved their glitter, like a mirror's face
Held to my revel with such flattering care.
And when it might have tarnished, with what grace
Moonlight, Waterlight, Opal were not there!

These moonbeam niceties, sweet to undergo,
Have been an austere discipline, the less
Exceptionable in that trifling so
I've learned to be content with nothingness.

THE DOWNWARD PULSE

Whether by choice or chance, with roving fondness
A mouth met mine, and I, from circling, dived –
Whether by choice or chance, mate of my blindness,
How steep a moment, to be manned and wived!

Blood beating in my head sang me towards ruin.
I broke sharp off into my former plane,
Abandoned that long, vertical self-wooing
And took to random circling once again.

The downward pulse still beats in me. The shiver
Plucks at my tendons and fatigues my flight.
Beware lest a numb, desperate twitch deliver
Me back again to that blood-roaring night.

THE SHACK

What trick or spell was on you, that you must
Choose one who had his house in lava-dust –
Me, the grey monster, arrogant and blind
To your home-making, a primeval kind?
I nudged your flowers and curtains all askew,
The harsh dust from my boots ate the floor through,
Made your home like a shack for engineers
Exiled in comfortless suspense for years
Until they can return to whence they came;
But you meant ever here, and I the same.

Though I am held, at least to frame good-bye:
On your behalf and mine to pay these dry
Respects to an eternal habitation
That choked you to death, child, with its desolation.

THE WANTON'S DEATH

She, wild with wantonness, to her two suitors,
A merman and a landman, gave this challenge:
'To prove his love the sturdier, each abandon
The element in which his suit was fostered
And undergo this test of transmutation,
Merman ashore, landman beyond the breakers.'
The two obeyed, in fear and pride and passion.
One gasped and writhed, the other choked and floundered;
She, to both quarters native, found them sporting.
At length each suitor found a spacious refuge,
Merman a pool, landman a reefy foothold,
Both claiming still the guerdon of achievement.
And, when she mocked their lie, each vowed in anger
His new-adapted element more kindly
Than the fair promiser who brought him thither . . .
Her relics rot on the sea-wasted foreshore,
Half-wooed, half-spurned by the land-tainted spindrift.

NOW LET ME ROLL

Now let me roll beneath the hooves of chance,
Though they may smash my members, heart or brain.
Worms live when severed – somewhere in the expanse
Of this long body dear life will remain:
Rather than lunge upright amongst the herd,
A face thrust up between the brutish backs,
Staring and yelling, desperate, absurd –
The brief last stand of *homo contumax*.

Life, the proud slattern, blandly will abide
Even in a prone or lacerated host;
But ridicule breaks in upon her pride,
With which she warms her lodging like a frost.
Then she, who any worm or pulp can cherish,
Amid that death of pride herself will perish.

THE FIRM OF HAPPINESS, LIMITED

The firm of Happiness, Limited, was one to astonish the stars,
More like a thriving town than a multiple store – a hotchpotch
Of markets and playrooms and chapels and brothels and
    baths and bars,
As smoothly running and closely packed as the works of
  a watch.

Nobody finally understood the cause of the crash.
Some spoke of Nemesis; others rumoured, vaguely, of course,
That a gang of Directors had simply robbed the firm of its cash,
Or that some ironical Jew was selling it short on the Bourse.

Whatever the reason, the firm of a sudden began to fail.
The floors were undusted at corners, the commissionaires
    were unshaved,
The girls were anxious and raucous, the comedian's jokes
    were stale.
The customers noticed the difference – to judge from the way
    they behaved.

When Happiness closed its doors, the Corporation of the city
Were distressed to see so vast a property left alone
To moulder and waste; in a mingled impulse of thrift and pity
They decided to buy the empty building, and floated a loan.

Now nobody knows what to do with this monstrous hulk we
    have bought.
At the last Corporation meeting one alderman, half in jest,
Spoke of turning it into a barracks. Meanwhile there's the
    dreary thought
That we ratepayers have to keep paying the burdensome
    interest.

A VISIT TO THE DEAD

I bought (I was too wealthy for my age)
A passage to the dead ones' habitat,
And learnt, under their tutelage,
To twitter like a bat

In imitation of their dialect.
Crudely I aped their subtle practices;
By instinct knew how to respect
Their strict observances.

The regions of the dead are small and pent,
Their movements faint, sparing of energy.
Yet, like an exiled Government,
With so much jealousy

As were the issue a campaign or Crown,
They hold debates, wage Cabinet intrigues,
Move token forces up and down,
Turn inches into leagues.

Long I was caught up in their twilit strife.
Almost they got me, almost had me weaned
From all my memory of life.
But laughter supervened:

Laughter, like sunlight in the cucumber,
The innermost resource, that does not fail.
I, Marco Polo, traveller,
Am back, with what a tale!

THE INVADER

Our shops and farms wide open lie;
Still the invader feels a lack:
Disquiet whets his gluttony
For what he may not carry back.

He prowls about in search of wealth
But has no skill to recognize
Our things of worth: we need no stealth
To mask them from his pauper eyes.

He calls for worship and amaze;
We give him yes-men in a row,
Reverberating that self-praise
He wearied of a while ago.

He casts around for some new whim,
Something preposterously more:
'Love me' he bids. We offer him
The slack embraces of a whore.

And when he spitefully makes shift
To share with us his pauperdom,
By forcing on us as a gift
The shoddy wares he brought from home,

And watches that we sell and buy
Amongst us his degrading trash,
He gets no gain at all. Though sly
With what he knows, the guns and cash,

What he knows not he may not touch:
Those very spoils for which he came
Are still elusive to his clutch –
They swerve and scorch him like a flame.

Invader–outcast of all lands,
He lives condemned to gorge and crave,
To foul his feast with his own hands:
At once the oppressor and the slave.

THE VOTIVE IMAGES

'Our deaths,' he said, 'share with us in our lives
And should be entertained with deference.
The man of sensitivity contrives
A room befitting death's own residence.'

The self-appointed steward of death's room,
He had not been aware of that evasion
Whereby, each moment he was spared from doom,
A votive image signalled the occasion,

Set in that very chamber. Ah, disgrace!
These life's heads, these *mementoes vivere*
Jostled and winked and chattered – made the place
As death-befitting as an aviary.

When he at last went in, stirrings still rife
Within the shroud woke their life-loyal thirst.
Guardian of life in death, of death in life,
They hailed him as King Sensitive the First.

THE DIRTY LITTLE ACCUSER

Who invited him in? What was he doing here,
That insolent little ruffian, that crapulous lout?
When he quitted a sofa, he left behind him a smear.
My wife says he even tried to paw her about.

What was worse, if, as often happened, we caught him out
Stealing or pinching the maid's backside, he would leer,
With a cigarette on his lip and a shiny snout,
With a hint: 'You and I are all in the same galère.'

Yesterday we ejected him, nearly by force,
To go on the parish, perhaps, or die of starvation;
As to that, we agreed, we felt no kind of remorse.

Yet there's this check on our righteous jubilation:
Now that the little accuser is gone, of course,
We shall never be able to answer his accusation.

GREEN, GREEN IS EL AGHIR

Sprawled on the crates and sacks in the rear of the truck,
I was gummy-mouthed from the sun and the dust of the track,
And the two Arab soldiers I'd taken on as hitch-hikers
At a torrid petrol-dump, had been there on their hunkers
Since early morning. I said, in a kind of French
'On m'a dit, qu'il y a une belle source d'eau fraîche,
Plus loin, à El Aghir' . . .

             It was eighty more kilometres
Until round a corner we heard a splashing of waters,
And there, in a green, dark street, was a fountain with
      two faces
Discharging both ways, from full-throated faucets
Into basins, thence into troughs and thence into brooks.
Our negro corporal driver slammed his brakes,
And we yelped and leapt from the truck and went at
      the double
To fill our bidons and bottles and drink and dabble.
Then, swollen with water, we went to an inn for wine.
The Arabs came, too, though their faith might have
      stood between.
'After all,' they said, 'it's a boisson,' without contrition.

Green, green is El Aghir. It has a railway-station,
And the wealth of its soil has borne many another fruit,
A mairie, a school and an elegant Salle de Fêtes.
Such blessings, as I remarked, in effect, to the waiter,
Are added unto them that have plenty of water.

VIA MAESTRANZA

There's curfew in this town: but all night long
Lovers and smugglers rove. I'm wakened by
Their paces or the clatter of their carts;
Sometimes 'Halt! Who goes there?' from the patrol,
Scurrying flight, a desultory shot
Fired more in duty than with aim to kill.
Then the patrol has passed, and life resumes.

We lodge upon the *piano nobile*,
The gentry's floor. The cornice of my room
Is decked with grinning faces in relief;
The tiled floor bears a large masonic sign.
And in this room a whisper down the street,
'Let me in, Pietro! Quickly, the patrol!'
Sounds loudly as though uttered by my bed.

STEEP STONE STEPS

Steep stone steps, stinking with washing water –
Italy inhales its incense, Dante's derelict daughter.
Poverty, Peter's Pence, politics, capital, conniving.
Thieves thwart the thankless struggler's stalwart striving:
Hard, hoarding husbandry doomed, daunted, defeated,
Master masons, metalworkers chidden, checked, cheated.
Rich rogues revel, frauds fatten: what wonder
Dignity departs, patriotism perishes, petty plunder,
Servile subterfuges spread social suppuration?
Nevertheless nature's high heart carries consolation:
Generosity, joy, gentleness, mankind's measureless mines,
Love, laughter lavishly live, sun shines.

THE VERDICT

It was taken a long time ago,
The first pressure on the trigger.
Why complain that the verdict is so?
It was taken a long time ago.
And our grave will have many a digger,
The Mongol, the Yank and the nigger.
It was taken a long time ago,
The first pressure on the trigger.

(near Imola, April 1945)

WÖRTHER SEE

Would that wars might end for all soldiers like this:
Swimming, rowing, sailing, deep walks in the woods;
Landscapes rich in vines and maize, flowers and fruit;
Natives clean and honest, plump, wooable girls;
Food well-cooked and varied, camp discipline light;
No more danger, boredom, dirt, weariness, din;
Pride in battles won, the world's gratitude earned;
Ease in which to stretch the cramped limbs of the soul:
Would that wars might end for all soldiers like this.

(Carinthia, Autumn 1945)

A HOOK FOR LEVIATHAN

'Why, yes, the works are busy on the hook
Designed to drag Leviathan from hiding.
"Not really mean it?" Why, man have a look!
Ten thousand tons of steel along the siding,

A billion cubic feet of foundry sand,
We've not collected all that stuff for play.
A project such as this, you'll understand,
Is not to be completed in a day.

Think of the huge machine-tools we'll employ
To cut the barbs: no metal's hard enough.
We're still kept waiting for the new alloy.
We'll have you know, Leviathan's jaws are tough.

Then there's the little matter of the line –
Unprecedented problem of suspension.
A million strands, we've learnt, would be too fine.
We're making fresh experiments in tension.'

And if you ask: 'Where will you find the vessel
To carry such a hook?' the owners stare:
'Surely we have enough with which to wrestle.
We're not ship-builders. That's not our affair.'

UNTITLED ALPHABET POEM

After
Beauty
Cometh
Death
Ev'ry
Flower
Gay
Hath
Its
Joyful
Kingdom
Lost –
Monarch
None
Obey.
Pleading
Queens
Reluctant
Shall
Tumble
Unto
Viewless
Ways,
eXiles
Yearning
Zombie-like . . .

LIBERATION IN VIENNA

Totalitarian Winter, Occupying Power!
Like savage troops in grimy battledress
His piles of dirty snow sit there and glower,
Holding the streets in terror and duress.

His agents know our tongue, our thoughts as well,
He warps our hearts and brains to his own shape.
No partisan of Summer dares rebel,
Feeling the frost's revolver on the nape.

But now the glorious legions of the sun
Assault the roof-tops – their El Alamein!
The formed platoons of Winter break and run,
Their dingy corpses tumble down the drain.

Winter is strong and crafty yet; by night
His Secret State Police make their patrols,
Whistling through crevices: 'We're here, all right.
Winter's not easily dislodged, good souls!'

Heap grapes and roses high on Summer's altar:
Winter is gone, with all his dreadful crew.
Yet still they have the words to make us falter:
'Wait, citizens, till Winter comes anew.'

A MODERN NIGHTMARE

When Satan finds a rebel in his realm,
He laces round the head of the poor fool
A frightful mask, a sort of visored helm
That has a lining soaked in vitriol.
The renegade begins to scream with pain.
(The mask is not designed to gag the sound,
Which propagates the terror of his reign.)
The screams come through the visor, but are drowned
By the great shouting of the overlord,
Who, in relaying them, distorts their sense
So that the cringing listeners record
Mere cries of villainy or penitence . . .
Yet Satan has a stronger hold: the fear
That, if his rule is threatened, he will tear
The mask from that pain-crazed automaton
And show his vassals just what he has done.

PUNISHMENT ENOUGH

They say that women, in a bombing-raid,
Retire to sleep in brand-new underwear
Lest they be tumbled out of doors, displayed
In shabby garments to the public stare.

You've often seen a house, sliced like a cheese,
Displaying its poor secrets – peeling walls
And warping cupboards. Of such tragedies
It is the petty scale that most appals.

When you confess your sins before a parson,
You find it no great effort to disclose
Your crimes of murder, bigamy and arson,
But can you tell him that you pick your nose?

If after death you pay for your misdeeds,
Surely the direst and most just requital
Would be to listen while an angel reads
Before a crowd your endless, mean recital:

Golf scorecards faked, thefts from your mother's purse . . .
But why should Doomsday bother with such stuff?
This is the Hell that you already nurse
Within you. You've had punishment enough.

BEAR IN MIND, O YE RECORDING ANGELS

Bear in mind, o ye recording angels,
That all of us, from the Pope to Stalin,
From Lavatory Dan to John D. Rockefeller,
Are children gazing in a sweetshop window.

LUCIFER

Lucifer did not wish to murder God,
But only to reduce His Self-esteem.
Weary of brightness where no shadow showed,
What took the rebel's fancy was a dream

Of God bewildered, angered out of measure
And driven, almost weeping, to implore,
'I built this Heaven for My angels' pleasure,
And yet you like it not. What would you more?'

At this, of course, with most Divine compassion,
Lucifer, all forgiving and adept,
Would soon have taught his Master how to fashion
A Heaven such as angels could accept.

NEVER MIND

Never mind if you have fallen into slavery to booze:
There's a novel Danish treatment that will cure you while
    you snooze.
Never mind if you're a selfish bore whom normal men avoid:
You'll get worshipful attention from some follower of Freud.
If your wife has run away because you make her want to retch,
Never mind, for there are plenty of good pebbles on the beach.
And if your body buckles up beneath its load of vice,
Never mind about the funeral: the State will pay the price.

'THAT WIERD SALL NEVER DAUNTON ME'

(Syne he hath kissed her rosy lips
All underneath the Eildon tree)

Aye, marry, will she, boastful Scot.
A kiss is not the fee
Will gar a wierd come share your lot
Like any other she.

Yet 'tis a she, whate'er may come,
With woman's round, fierce eyes.
She hath a womb, and ilka womb
Doth teem with greed and lies.

She'll daunton thee and drag thee down
In worship and despair,
In sorry self-negation
Hating thyself in her.

If thou a wierd wilt rightly woo,
Kiss not, and hush thy mirth,
For firstly must thou undergo
The pangs of a new birth.

Thy resurrection then is hers;
She showeth another face,
A woman still, but unawares,
And dowered with faery grace;

And thou canst woo her not afear'd –
Or poets thus do say.
But, ah! what suitor of a wierd
Hath lived to tell the day?

BLACK TAKES WHITE

On the Italian front there was a sector
That neither side had any great respect for.
Jerry looked down from a west-Apennine hill-mass
That one brigade could hold from now to Christmas,
While, for attack, he had no troops to squander.
In fact, the show was largely propaganda:
The Yanks had negroes, Jerry had Italians,
In regular divisions and battalions
To prove that they were pukka fighting allies;
Though plainly neither mob had any relish
For warfare (and why should they, lacrima Christi!
Negroes for Jays, peasants for squadristi?)
The only major movement in those quarters
Was a dense, two-way traffic of deserters.

It chanced that a deserting negro party
Encountered a like-minded Eytie.
At this a keen discussion was engendered,
Each party claiming that it had surrendered
And that the other had become its captor.
The Eyties held the trump, the winning factor:
Their lot was led by an uffiziale;
What *he* said, went. (The tale's a tribute, really,
To both sides' rather narrow sense of duty.)
Back marched the negroes with their unsought booty.

Imagine how the P.R.O.'s got cracking!
Here was the feat of arms they'd long been lacking.
Nobody paused to bother with such trifles
As where the captors had mislaid their rifles.
Quickly these fed-up and embarrassed negroes
Were praised, promoted, given gongs as heroes,
And photographs of their victorious battle
Were published from Long Island to Seattle.

III
Juvenilia

DISEASE OF THE MIND

Mad as the jabbering thing that cries
    As it hangs, bat-like, from the pine,
Choking and dank as the mist in my eyes,
    Blood-red, where weird things shine,
Gross as the flesh of the graveyard worm
    Swelled fat with the dread plague's toll, –
Such are my thoughts, while the madness germ
    Comes, sickens my labouring soul.
'Gods!' as I strike with quivering hate,
    At the air which, clinging and wet,
Binds me around like the shroud of fate,
    Or a spider's blood-stained net,
Tortured am I. Set free, I pray,
    This struggling spirit of mine,
Freed from the foul flesh, let it stray
    In the wind and the clean sunshine.

THE DEATH-BED OF P. AELIUS HADRIANUS IMPERATOR

Animula vagula blandula
hospes comesque corporis,
quae nunc abibis in loca
pallidula rigida nudula,
nec ut soles dabis iocos!

> The Oxford Book
> of Latin Verse

......

'Little soul, gentle and wandering,
This body's most loyable guest,
Whither away, pale, cold, and forlorn,
Small sprite of the whimsical jest?'

So the emperor called; at the rich curtains
Felt the groping fingers of day;
But no faint, troubled cry came through the darkness
From his soul on its pale-winged way.

......

A mouse, with timid inquisitiveness,
Ran over the emperor's chin,
For he heard no sound from the emperor's breast
Of the small, dead mouse within.

THEOCRITUS: A TRANSLATION

Idyll VIII.55, 56

'But here beneath the shadow of this rock
I'll lie and sing and in my arms hold thee,
Whilst there our sheep are grazing as one flock
And yonder dreams the sea of Sicily.'

A SONG

They go between sun-dappled trees,
When green woods are shady,
Do Acme and Septimius,
The lover and his lady,
When green woods are shady.

And who could find a loving pair
More blessed, howe'er essayed he,
Than Acme and Septimius,
The lover and his lady,
When green woods are shady?

A BOWL OF WINE

(11 p.m. Midsummer)

As green as shallow water lay the sky
(With clouds like purple fishes flitting by),
    Save where, to North,
    Strange lights flared forth.
Two hills enclasped a huge, transparent bowl
Of wine, with crimson dregs like living coal.

I thought to straddle o'er the mountain-line
And take tremendous pulls at that great wine.
    But whoso quaffed
    That splendid draught
Could trundle echoing moons around in play,
Like snowballs gathering stars upon their way.

DWELLERS IN THE SEA

My soul is some leviathan in vague distress
That travels up great slopes of hills beneath the sea.
   Up from the darkness and the heaviness
   Into a slowly gathering radiancy.
But wiser now, alas! to plunge and swim away;
For if he burst upon that mystic light of day,
   Leviathan must gasp in lack of breath
   And find what dwellers in the sea call death.
We hapless dwellers in the sea cannot be told,
No brave leviathan has ever back returned
   To tell us how stupendous mountains rolled
   Like porpoises, beneath a sky that burned,
How unimaginable light along his scales
Changed colour, till Leviathan was mailed in glory.
   We have but rumours, unsubstantial tales;
   And who would give his life up for a story?

IN AN ATTIC BEDROOM

Do they, then, hold me in such vast esteem
    In this hotel?
They chose me out, so it would seem,
    For some great entomologist at will

To scan through microscopes my countenance,
    Perhaps to hear
My curious human utterance.
    (Is that indeed a huge, attentive ear

With Jabberwocky hand held funnel-wise,
    Or must it change,
Wind-blown, and take some other guise
    With outline too fantastically strange

For even dream-struck probability?)
    Type of my race,
Poor panic-stricken deputy
    I lurk – inside this glassy, roofed-in case.

Is there for me a jar among the rest,
    The fauna of this world,
Each in his pint of spirit pressed,
    Eyes bulging, limbs uncomfortably curled,

Meek specimen of homo sapiens?
    What thoughts oppress
The brain behind that monstrous lens,
    What wormy thoughts of death and dustiness?

THE MARSH OF AGES

The marsh of ages that a man may find
Deep in his mind,
It has a musty and an antique breath,
Being rank with death.
And yet in ancient times this was a mere
Fresh-water-clear,
Where monsters like great lumps of ambergris
Floated at peace.
Now all those early-time iguanodons
Are skeletons,
That sleep on their own droppings underneath;
And scissor-teeth,
Whose lightest graze could start a jet of blood,
Are gulphed in mud.
On top are piled the beasts of every age,
By stage on stage
And layer on layer, up to the outer rind
Of lessening kind,
Until their corpses choke up all the fen.
No wonder, then,
So putrid rich with fertilizing time
The ancient slime
Makes keen as knives and coarse as canvas is
The rank grasses.
No wonder, then, the fen-fire dragons spy,
With necks awry
And hanging, wavering heads, like flowers on stalks,
On him who walks
Across the marshy surface – who must fear
These phantoms, mere
Children of vapours rising from the bed
Of dragons dead.

PEACE FROM GHOSTS

Wherever men have dwelt
Ghosts, though not felt,
Are thronging round in emptiness always,
Ghosts of old miseries
And agonies,
The haggard storm-rack of disastrous days;
Pains that extinguished life
By surgeon's knife,
Humiliations of poor, cheated brides
Impressed on empty air,
Vibrating there,
Dash to and fro on violent, short tides,
Tossing without a rest
At her behest,
Cold moon of universal sufferings.

But what has he to do with ghostly things,
The man who is laid here
Inside this bier,
From all those sad or glorious visionings,
That filled or broke his heart,
A thing apart,
Less meaning than an empty cartridge-case;
While underneath the steeple
Some quiet people
With courteous, unsignifying grace
Most decorously lay
Him dead away.
No tides of trouble wash against these coasts.
For surely trouble free
Must graveyards be,
The only places where there are no ghosts.

IV

Selections from

François Villon, Poems

Translated to the Original Verse-Forms

from THE BEQUESTS

or THE LITTLE TESTAMENT

I

In the year fourteen fifty-six,
I, Francis Villon, *clericus*,
Serenely now my purpose fix,
To celebrate that ancient use
Recorded by Vegetius
(Sage Roman, mighty counseller),
Profession *coram omnibus*,
Sans which a man is wont to err.

II

It was upon th' aforesaid date,
Near the dead season of Noël,
When wolves have only wind for meat,
And men close by the fireside dwell,
Out of the frost's benumbing spell,
I had a sudden wish to break
The very am'rous prison-cell
Wherein my heart so long did ache.

III

And I accomplish'd my intent
By seeing Her, before my eyes,
Giving my ruin her consent,
What though it brought her little prize:
Wherefore I mourn, and beg the skies
And all the gods of venery
For vengeance on her for my sighs
And easement of my agony.

IV

And if I thought they boded well,
Her sugar'd looks and fairest shows,
Which, though they were as false as Hell,
Could pierce my entrails – as for those,
They pay no scot for all my woes
And fail me in my direst need.
On other breasts I'll seek repose,
In other gardens plant my seed.

V

Her glance hath ta'en me prisoner,
She who hath so ill-served me,
What though I did no wrong to her;
She seeks and bids that I should dree
The pangs of death, and no more be.
I see no help but to begone.
She tears her branch from my live tree,
And doth not hear my piteous moan!

VI

To spare myself a mortal wound,
'Tis best, I reckon, to depart.
Farewell! For Angers I am bound,
Since unto me she'll not impart
Her favour, no, nor any part.
Through her I die, with body whole;
And thus I canonize my heart,
A martyr on the saintly roll!

VII

Sore though the parting give me grief,
I nothing can, I must begone;
As my poor wits compel belief,
Another shelters 'neath her gown;
And ne'er a herring of Boulogne
Was parch'd with saltier spleen than I.
A piteous task I'm set upon:
May God be pleas'd to hear my cry!

PETITION TO MY LORD OF BOURBON

Mine own liege lord and most revered prince,
Flow'r of the Lily, of right royal blood,
Your servant Francis Villon, who doth wince
Beneath the blows of Fortune, oft renew'd,
Hereby beseeches that you think it good
To favour him with some small, gracious loan,
An obligation he will ne'er disown;
Doubt not that you shall have it back entire:
With neither loss nor interest thereon,
'Twill cost you but the time of waiting, Sire.

No other prince nor lord nor Eminence
Hath he in life for such a favour woo'd.
Those half a dozen crowns you lent, long since
He hath expended solely for his food.
Both debts he'll pay at once, be't understood;
Nay, more, he'll pay them easily and soon.
If acorns yet around Patay are grown,
And if men still set chestnuts on the fire,
You shall have certain restitutiòn:
'Twill cost you but the time of waiting, Sire.

If I could sell my health for a few pence
To any of the Lombard brotherhood,
I do believe I'ld seize upon the chance,
So much doth lack of money vex my mood.
Cash have I none, in purse or tunic stow'd.
'Fore God! I never see a cross nor crown,
Unless it be a cross of wood or stone.
I vow and promise, let me but acquire
Such crosses as my heart is set upon,
'Twill cost you but the time of waiting, Sire.

Prince, fam'd for leaving no good deed undone,
Think you how sore it makes your servant moan
When all his hopes are trampled in the mire?
Hear me, and, if it please you, grant this boon:
'Twill cost you but the time of waiting, Sire.

from THE TESTAMENT

or THE GREAT TESTAMENT

I

In this my thirtieth year of age
I've drunk the dregs of my disgrace,
Not all a fool, nor all a sage,
Sharp lessons though I've had to face,
Each of which sev'rally I trace
Back unto Tybalt d'Auxigny:
A bishop, he, in pride and place –
That he be mine, I do deny!

II

No lord of mine nor bishop, he;
If land I hold of him, 'tis waste;
I owe him neither faith nor fee;
I'm not his vassal nor his beast.
Water and crusts were all my feast
A summer long: captive or free,
From his oppression ne'er released:
God be to him as he to me!

III

And here, if any should upbraid
And say, I utter calumnies,
Not so! If well the thing is weigh'd,
'Tis seen I slander him no wise.
Here's all the burden of my cries:
If he to me was merciful,
Sweet Jesus, King of Paradise,
Be so to him, body and soul!

IV

And if on me he harshly trod,
Far more than I do here recount,
I pray that the Eternal God
May serve him likewise on this count!
The Church here calls us to account,
And bids us all for foes to pray.
I'll eat my words: the full amount
Of what he did, let God assay!

V

Yes, I'll pray for him, by the shroud
Of good old Cotart! But, beware!
For utterance of prayers aloud
I have but little breath to spare.
I'll say for him a Picard's prayer;
And, if he doth remember ill
What that may be, let him repair
To Douai, or to Flemish Lille!

VI

Yet if he truly seek to know
What prayer I'll say, then, by my Creed!
Since 'tis a favour he is slow
To ask, I shall supply his need.
I'll take my Psalter, which, indeed,
Is not bedeck'd with gold or gem,
And there the seventh verse I'll read
Out of the Psalm, *Deus laudem.*

VII

Thus do I pray to God's dear Son,
To whom I cry in all my dole;
And may my piteous orison
Reach Him who gave me flesh and soul;
Who in His grace hath kept me whole
From many a hurt and vile mischance.
Him and Our Lady we extol,
And Louis, the good King of France!

Ballade of the Ladies of bygone time

Tell me but where, beneath what skies
Is lovely Roman Flora ta'en?
Tell me where Archipiada lies,
Or Thais (they were kin, these twain);
Or Echo, answering again
Across the river and the mere,
Beauty of more than human strain?
Where are the snows of yesteryear?

Where is the learned Eloise,
For whom Pierre Abelard, her swain,
Became a monk at Saint Denis,
And had for her his manhood slain?
Where is the queen who did ordaïn
That Buridan, her sometime dear,
Should perish coldly in the Seine?
Where are the snows of yesteryear?

Queen Blanche, white as a fleur-de-lys,
Who sang like sirens o'er the main?
Bertha the Broadfoot, Beatrice,
Or Erembourg who held the Maine;
Or Joan, sweet lady of Lorraine,
For whom the English drop no tear:
Where are they, Virgin sovereign?
Where are the snows of yesteryear?

Prince, do not ask where they are lain,
Ask not the week, ask not the year,
Lest you remember this refrain:
Where are the snows of yesteryear?

The lament of the fair Heaulmière

Methinks I hear the harlot wail
Who was the helmet-maker's lass,
Wishing herself still young and hale,
And crying in her woe: 'Alas!
Old Age, so cruel and so crass,
Why hast thou struck me down so soon?
What holds me back that, in this pass,
I do not seek death's final boon?

'Hast robb'd me of that mighty sway
Which beauty gave me at my birth
O'er all men, clerical or lay.
Once there was not a man on earth
But would have given all his worth,
Could he but win of me that prize
Which now, in these my days of dearth,
Even the beggars do despise.

'There's many a man I could have had,
But flouted, in my foolishness,
For love of a sharp-witted lad
On whom I shower'd my largesse.
Others might buy a feign'd caress:
'Twas he I lov'd, more than myself,
Whom he did cruelly oppress,
And lov'd me only for my pelf.

'And yet his bitterest attack
Could never cause my love to die.
He could have dragg'd me on my back
Or trampled me – did he but cry
"Kiss me!" away my woes would fly.
That beast, that slimy manikin,
Would cuddle me . . . And what have I
Left for it all? Disgrace and sin!

'Well, thirty years ago he died,
And I am left here, old and hoar.
When I bethink my days of pride,
What I am now, and was of yore,
Or when I hold a glass before
My naked body, now so chang'd,
Wrinkled and shrunken, frail and poor,
My wits with grief are nigh estrang'd.

'Where is that forehead's fair expanse;
That golden hair; those arching brows;
Those wide-set eyes; that pretty glance,
With which I charm'd the most morose;
Those little ears; that dainty nose,
Neither too tiny nor too great;
That dimpled chin; those Cupid's bows
Of lips; those teeth so white and straight?

'Where are the shoulders neat and slender;
Those long, soft arms; those fingers brent;
Those little breasts; those haunches tender,
High-rais'd and smooth and plainly meant
For riders in love's tournament;
Those ample loins, firm thighs, and twat
Set like a graceful monument
Within its handsome garden-plot?

'The forehead scowls, the hair is grey,
The brows are gone, the eyes are blear
That were so mocking and so gay
They fill'd the passers-by with cheer;
The nose is hook'd and far from fair,
The ears are rough and pendulous,
The face is sallow, dead and drear,
The chin is purs'd, the lips hang loose.

'Aye, such is human beauty's lot!
The arms are short; the hands clench tight;
The shoulders tangle in a knot;
The breasts, in shame they shrink from sight;
Nipple and haunch, they share their plight;
The twat – ah, bah! The thighs are thin
As wither'd hams, and have a blight
Of freckles, like a sausage-skin.

''Tis thus we mourn for good old days,
Perch'd on our buttocks, wretched crones,
Huddled together by the blaze
Of some poor fire of forest cones,
That dies as quickly as our moans,
A briefly-lit, brief-living flame –
We who have sat on lovers' thrones! . . .
With many a man 'tis just the same.'

A ballade in prayer to Our Lady

Lady of Heav'n, God's Regent over man
And Empress over the infernal mere,
Receive Thou me, Thine humble Christian,
That I may dwell with them thou holdest dear,
Though naught at all have I deserved here.
Such grace as Thine, Lady and Governess,
Doth far outweigh my human sinfulness;
That grace sans which (I know, and tell no lie)
No soul can e'er aspire to saintliness.
'Tis in this faith I mean to live and die.

Say to Thy Son, I serve him as I can,
That He may cause my sins to disappear,
As once He pardon'd the Egyptian,
Or eke that cleric whom He did not ban
From mercy, but Thy plea for him did hear,
What though the Devil held him in duress.
Preserve Thou me from such a wickedness,
Virgin who bore, in unstain'd sanctity,
The Host we duly celebrate at Mass.
'Tis in this faith I mean to live and die.

I'm but a poor old woman, small and wan;
Naught have I read, of naught am well aware.
In church the painted images I scan
Of Paradise, and also of a drear
Place where the wicked boil: these make me fear,
Those others give me joy and happiness.
Grant that the joy be mine, Thou Holiness
To Whose protection sinners all should fly;
Crown me with faith, sans feint or idleness:
'Tis in this faith I mean to live and die.

V irgin who bore, most virtuous princess,
J esus whose reign o'er men shall never cease,
L ord who assum'd our mortal feebleness,
L eft Heav'n and to succour us drew nigh,
O ffering death his young, sweet loveliness.
N ow such Our Lord is, such I him confess.
'Tis in this faith I mean to live and die.

Lay

Death, of thy rigour I complain:
Hast ravished my mistress hence,
And wilt not yet show penitence,
But holdest me in swooning pain,
With all my vital forces ta'en.
How did her life give thee offence,
    Death?

We had one heart between the twain:
If she be dead, it follows thence
That I must die, or in pretence
Live on, like images that feign
    Death!

The ballade of Fat Margie

If I do serve my love with all my heart,
Must you, then, take me for a rogue or sot?
For certain charms she hath no counterpart.
With her I am a very Lancelot:
When people come, I run to drink a pot,
I 'go for wine' with soft and nimble tread,
I fetch them water, cheese and fruit and bread,
If they pay well, I cry them: '*Bene stat*;
Pray come again, when you've a load to shed,
To this bordèl where we are thron'd in state!'

But afterwards a bitter brawl may start,
When Margie comes back home without a groat.
Then hatred of her stabs me like a dart;
I seize her gown, her girdle and her coat
And swear I'll sell them all to pay her scot;
Whereat she screams, with arms akimbo spread,
And swears, by all the living and the dead,
It shall not be! And then I seize a slat
And score her face with notches fiery red,
In this bordèl where we are thron'd in state.

Then peace is made and she lets flee a fart,
Like an envenom'd beetle all a-bloat,
And lays her hand upon my privy part.
'Go, go!' she cries, and smites my tender spot.
Both drunk, we slumber like a worn-out boot.
At dawn her rumbling stomach wakes her greed;
She mounts me, eager not to waste my seed.
I groan beneath her, flatten'd by her weight,
Until the very life of me is sped,
In this bordèl where we are thron'd in state.

Come wind, come hail, come frost, I've bak'd my bread.
A lecher to a lecheress is wed.
Which is the worse? There's little to be said.
Like unto like: 'Bad cat for a bad rat.'
We love the mire, and miry is our bed;
We flee from honour, honour now is fled,
In this bordèl where we are thron'd in state.

VILLON'S EPITAPH

Men, brothers whom we shall not see again,
Let not your hearts towards us be unkind;
For if you pity us poor men and plain,
God's mercy unto you will be inclin'd.
Here you behold some six of us alin'd.
Our flesh, that we did all too well supply,
Did long since shrivel up and putrefy,
And we, the bones, to dust and ashes fall.
Let none make sport of our adversity,
But pray to God that he forgive us all!

We call you brothers. Nay, do not disdain
The kinship, though it was by seal'd and sign'd
Mandate of law that we poor six were slain:
Not all men always are of righteous mind.
Now we are dead, we've left our sins behind;
So plead with Jesus that his charity
Towards us erring sheep may not run dry,
But save us from the flame perpetual.
We're dead, no soul torments us inwardly;
But pray to God that he forgive us all!

We have been wash'd and purified by rain;
The sun hath burnt us to a blacken'd rind;
The crows and magpies have dug out our eyen;
Eyebrows and beard are from our faces twin'd.
We have no rest: always the changing wind
Hunteth us to and fro, now low, now high.
Our skins are pitted like a strawberry
Where birds have peck'd them. Ye who would forestall
Such vengeance, be not of our company,
But pray to God that he forgive us all!

Jesus, who over all hast mastery,
Guard us from Satan's wicked signory:
He hath no rightful claim on us nor call.
Mankind, this is no place for mockery;
But pray to God that he forgive us all!

JE SUIS FRANÇOIS . . .

Francis by name, France's by birth
(I've never had much luck on earth),
At Paris first I op'd my eyes
(It is a hamlet near Pontoise);
And soon my neck, to end the farce,
Must learn how heavy is my arse.

V
Other Translations

HISTORICAL PICTURE

TRANSLATED FROM THE CZECH OF
VÍTĚZSLAV NEZVAL
WITH JIŘI MUCHA

Whilst the crowd continually shifts along the streets
Empty features mirroring the lamp posts' hollow struts
Over the laments from town to town a voice orates

Night's umbrella rises over hands together clasping
Pitchy wreaths of mingled stars and rain come downward
    slipping
All the bells in all the towns the angelus are lisping

A monotonous and silent voice makes ceaseless prayer
To the crowds that in their hurry stop and peer
Up the darkened alleys though the rain and anguish pour

Heads of women that the rain has moulded like a clout
Heads of city women tightly huddled to a clot
Hear with dread the voice that prays unto no paraclete

Whilst somewhere a message goes by galloping night-rider
Whilst the gates shut to behind the envious marauder
Whilst afar the rifle-bolt rings out surrender render

Whilst the sun sets and the strains of the Hail Mary steer
Through the city a procession headed by a star
To the roar of angry organs in the rain astir

Whilst a golden-headed woman silently discourses
With the enigmatic ghost beneath the lit-up crosses
Still disaster closes closes closes closes closes

In the ancient inn that history long since forsook
Where no mercenary sleeps now on a straw-stuffed sack
In the mediaeval inn with timbers grimed by smoke

From the oven-hole another voice begins to scoff
Reservoir and dyke are broken Nobody is safe
Save yourself each one who can yourself yourself yourself

Whilst the heavy heads of the companions sink and tremble
Heads of veterans each head bowed down with weight
    and trouble
See a shaggy hand lifts crosses over the card-table

Like the thief abroad the wind has struck the candles blind
Through the inn the doors lock of themselves The birds are
    limed
Thirty basses hoarsely utter land our land our land

From the stables suddenly there comes the muffled clank
Of a troop of horsemen Hooves and bridles click and clink
Glasses glasses calls the landlord twelve o'clock o'clock

Heads of veterans each head as heavy as an iron casque
Heads on the oak tables heads that meditations cark
Hear the din of spinning-wheels aroar and bolts acreak

After midnight with their locks aflutter on the stairs
They can hear like corpses rotting under evil stars
Daughters and descendants screaming to their ancestors

Since the dawn the bells have tolled above the black tail-coats
Over flag-poles tugging at the clouds with their regrets
Children by the locked-up school no longer fly their kites·

Children clutch their dogs and cower in dread they cower
At the sight of their own fathers dressed all black and queer
This day is the day when wounds are difficult to cure

This is the day when illnesses take graver turns
'Midst a dirge that's sung to kneeling villages and towns
Dogs and old men prick their ears to danger's overtones

Whilst a messenger who gallops on a sweating beast
Grunts head fallen forward till his chin is on his breast
One year past just one year past just one year past year past

Since the dawn in all cathedrals organs have been snarling
At the founder's grave a sable cloud of grief is kneeling
And the bell is knelling knelling knelling knelling knelling

Wound unspeakable this anniversary of wound
Women's eyes are wet and old men's faces drawn and wanned
Birdless weathervanes are turning where there is no wind

This day is the day when a new messenger takes reign
Messenger whose hair is grey and utterance a groan
Ruin ruin ruin ruin ruin ruin ruin

From the depths of night a portal's turning hinges wail
And a muffled tenor shouts beneath the castle wall
But the sentry answers silence silence sleep all's well

Afterwards the bolt upon the portal creaks and stirs
In a mask the night-time prowler hastens up the stairs
As the churches' clocks are chiming five upon the towers

Every sentry grasps his firelock in an anxious fist
Cocking half an eye towards the castle's central fort
Each one mutters to himself let's fight let's fight let's fight

In deep night before the gate six ruffians have bawled
Filthy curses at the raven that has croaked abroad
Things look bad look bad look bad look bad look bad look bad

Somewhere a hand vainly clenches in a frantic grip
From a mouth that hardly speaks for pain the two words drop
Over and again a trap a trap a trap a trap

On the staircase the accursed shadows reel in swoons
Like conspirators beneath the weight of their own sins
With the words his blood on us on us and on our sons

Now already in the city squares the people cram
Whilst the speaking-trumpet begs them calm be calm be calm
Just be quiet and disperse you see it had to come

Through the crowd from mouth to mouth dismaying
   rumours whirl
Fists are brandished from amongst the thousands toe to heel
Someone's strangled throat is calling hail all hail all hail

This becomes a cry that like a startled night-owl flits
Past the open window and the candle-flame that floats
In a haze of tears from eyelids like pale violets

In the barns the harvest is locked up with seven locks
Winter crops are scarce in fields that no man overlooks
Dusky fields on which the curse of someone nameless lurks

Crowds assemble round a voice that calls to them like chicks
Gather and disperse with hanging heads and burning cheeks
Fleeing from the voice that calls to them O Czechs O Czechs

Now they pass into a wakeful sleep with foreheads drooped
On wood settles stained where candle-wax and tears have
   dripped
Whilst a wailing from the sleepers' throats tells what they
   dreamt

On the walls decaying crosses crumble into flakes
Crosses at whose open wounds the tongue of morning licks
Nodding heads depressed by their own weight sink and relax

This day is a day that since the dawn has been bespelled
In the shops on such a day the curtains are not pulled
Soon beware upon our midst the comet will be spilled

Wives are busy changing-over wicks in all the lamps
On their husbands' uniforms they're ironing the loops
Sisters fit the masks around their younger brothers' lips

Fires are smouldering in barrels of the pointing guns
Smouldering awhile before the final blaze begins
In the black gun-barrels of the aimed and pointing guns

This day is a day when people do not lock their doors
Waiting as if midnight called them out to secret tours
This day is a day that's not for laughter or for tears

Men move in the streets like actors in a silent scene
Only with their hands exchanging gestures few discern
This day is the coming-true of every secret sign

The insistent signal of the harp calls folk from slumber
In the darkness flails and Hussite dirks and lances glimmer
The terrific comet nears watch over us Redeemer

From the speaking-trumpet once again the password's clanging
Men are leaving wives and grandams to their armchairs clinging
Up above the darkened town a vaulted sky is climbing

In the darkness men are folding up their dreadful gear
Linen still exhaling scents of soap and lavender
Saying as they leave this is the hour the hour the hour

On the dreadful hush a multitude in movement breaks
Feet are leaping into stirrups over saddles over brooks
Men today recall the prophecies in ancient books

In dead towns beneath the stars is heard a voice of woe
Ah my God how long a road my God how long a way
Or a secret whisper only war war war war war

Now they bar the windows with black paper-strips and paste
Bluish lamps grow pale beneath the sky's bright palimpsest
And a bat and after it another bat glides past

Little lamps are flickering between the carriage-wheels
Horses' hooves like jack-o'-lanterns scare the dogs to wails
Dogs are wailing at the planets wailing at the owls

In the hush one hears the water stir behind the tap
Creaking of a turning key or creaking of a step
Strangers on their way to death salute and do not stop

In the darkened houses where the bluish lighting winks
Broken families reform their decimated ranks
On this night the combs again begin to give off sparks

On this night the stars again absorb the pristine glamour
Of the new-made universe laid out before its framer
On this strangled night of stars this night of late September

Towns tonight are filled wth howling of the dogs the strays
That from woody mountain hamlets tracked their masters'
    spoors
Dogs that howled on village greens howl in the city squares

Through the lightless town a woman searches everywhere
After someone who by more than name was known to her
Through the stone-pale night she wanders with her golden hair

Vainly signing to the phantom of a coach that passes
Vainly signing to the dogs whose howling never pauses
Vainly signing to the clocks from which the midnight pulses

Now a row of houses seems to reel and overturn
Through the ruined kitchens and the roots of trees uptorn
She pursues the coachman to the quarry by the town

Running past the brick-kilns and across the hills afar
With a crowd of terrible companions to her fear
Hiding in the haystacks that the stars have set afire

Running like a maniac through villages and barns
Running from the image of destruction in her brains
Running with a torch of hair that burns and burns and burns

God why have you brought upon Your Nazareth this trouble?
Whilst our sisters keep the hospitals the cards will tumble
Brothers to decide your fate upon a green baize table

Innocent and guilty all alike shall be condemned
You have no recourse against a verdict preordained
Winds are shuffling through the cards whose issue is
    foredoomed

Here's the end of tourneys and Olympic festivals
Gnashing teeth can't stop the dreadful creaking of the quills
That shall bring unheard-of sadness on the land of Wales

Still monotonously creaking runs each rusty pen
Brothers all our country's ancient honour is in pawn
You have formed your battle lines in vain in vain in vain

Your historic raven croaks again you have been warned
Thrice the man has wept aloud and thrice the woman swooned
Woe upon the traitor in whose toils you have been wound

You should seek in vain the rogue who led you thus astray
Hanged beneath the tree of night upon the gallows-tree
'Tis a ghost who weeps not for his bloody sophistry

'Tis a ghost who at this hour is making a good meal
Of applause for his sweet farce that made the war-gods smile
He is bringing home his laurels seated on a mule

From the fields the roughly hooded heavy wagons rumble
They are straggling back with lamps extinguished in a rabble
Drinkers curse and thump the beer-drenched tables till they
    tremble

Underneath the hoods the company with shame half-wild
Waits whilst elsewhere and by someone else its fate is willed
Hush young nomads this is not the end of all the world

In the streets the tramped mud begins to spurt and boil
Like the blood where now they're busy slaughtering the bull
Even the beggar swallows down his quid in a tight ball

Vainly now the crowd gathers round the voice that calls
    its chicks
Gather and disperse with hanging heads and burning cheeks
Fleeing from the voice that calls to them O Czechs O Czechs

Vainly now the fists are brandished from a thousand sleeves
Vainly now in every square they gather in conclaves
'Tis the end of hope the end the end of all one loves

Whilst across the land the evening throws a dusky crimson
Hidden voices call towards the desolate horizon
Treason treason treason treason treason treason treason

Horses without masters now along the streets are roving
Horses with their stable doors left open for the reiving
Wander to the fields to hear the croaking of the raven

Other horses in their stalls prick up their ears and sidle
At the touch of trembling hands that fasten on the saddle
For the last time they shall see the land that was their cradle.

Village streets take on the semblance of a market-fair
Tears of the departing exiles fall upon the dead hearth-fire
As they lead their children off in search of homes afar

That's the end now of a human grief that's had no peer
Through a land without a flag the chilly breezes pour
On the tears of people who have learnt what is despair

Regiments without their flags or arms or discipline
Straggle back across the moribund September plain
That's the end of every grief the end of every plan

Ancient glory comes back home upon the killer's shield
Haughty teeth dig into lips The father with a chilled
Last embrace upon this day casts arms about his child

Soon his voice drowns in the whispers of his living tomb
Whilst a nation's folk are asking what will come of them
And the echo answers time and time and time and time

ODE TO BOMBED LONDON

TRANSLATED FROM THE FRENCH OF
PHILIPPE SOUPAULT

Tonight London is being bombed for the hundredth time.
Night, black night of murder and anger,
The darkness swells with the anguish to come.
Already the first strokes in the distance
And already the first flames, the first signals.
All seems ready for trouble, for trembling, for fear.
Everyone, suddenly silent, harks for the now familiar sounds.
Waiting for blind death's great festival,
A near, high, blazing brightness,
Dawn of a new world from the womb of night.

We were gagged with mud and unclean things;
We could still listen and wait.
We knew it, we guessed it,
London tonight is being bombed for the hundredth time.
A voice arose, it was the call we hoped for,
Ici Londres, Parla Londra, London calling.
We were silent as when one hears the beat of a heart.

Suddenly silence and the anguish of silence,
The time gone by, a second, an hour.
It is vain to enquire of night, of darkness and distance,
It is wrong to believe what the others are shouting:
London tonight is being bombed for the hundredth time,
A silent pyre of the men now dead,
Those men who called to us, those whom we awaited,
Nothing but the image of broken pylons and cut wires,
Nothing but this hole in space and time.

Ici Londres, Parla Londra, London calling,
And here is the City again in her place on the horizon.
She is alone at the centre of the world,
She it is who masters the tumult,
Lit by the blaze and the taller flame of courage,
London, London, London, always London,
Tonight London is being bombed for the hundredth time.

The attack and the answer, a defiance across the earth,
The voice that calls through infinity,
The voice of London like a friend at your bedside.
She says that one must not despair,
That she is rising in the hour of danger and shame.
She speaks of life to the moribund, of faith to those
    who doubt.
We listen, shutting our eyes, we know
Tonight London is being bombed for the hundredth time.

Courage, this is the hundredth night of courage.
The capital city of hope calls and recalls us;
The capital is the same as aforetime,
She who despises indifference, cowardice, baseness.
Now we follow her good old ghosts,
Thomas Dekker gliding from tavern to tavern
And Thomas de Quincey drinking the sad, sweet poison
    of opium
To his poor Anne, on his dreamy way
Tonight when London is being bombed for the hundredth
    time.

Ghosts and my youth spent near the docks,
London, you who dwell impassive as the stars,
Braving the conflagration and the fire-drunk wind
When two-thirds of your houses were burnt,
When the plague was raging from door to door
And men were dying by thousands,
A thousand and then a thousand and then a thousand anew,
Women and children first,
Ghosts of London and my youth, you appear
Tonight when London is being bombed for the hundredth
    time.

I emerge from my nocturnal paralysis
And glide like a memory, like a butterfly
Towards the familiar streets where the river's reflections
    guide me,
To that Monument that has no other name,
On that gloomy little square near the Elephant;

And there is a smiling young man whom I recognize
And who is, after all, the same man, since I live again
Tonight when London is being bombed for the hundredth
    time.

Today, after so many hoped-for and wasted years,
Condemned to the slavish silence of slaves,
I listen to this voice come from the depths of courage,
Which says and says again, echo of echoes,
He laughs best who laughs last,
As every evening before the dance-music,
Whilst the sirens are bellowing,
I hear, we hear, and the world with us,
The call, the same call and in the same voice,
The voice that expects that every man will do his duty
When London is being bombed for the hundredth time.

Every man does his duty, every single one,
Every man and every woman, every child,
Those who hasten to meet the flames,
Those who run in search of spilt blood,
Those who fly towards death,
Those women who weep or who smile,
Those who hold out their hands and hope,
All those who die without complaining
Now that London is being bombed for the hundredth time.

At the end of the world and of night
Those who are not afraid to die
Salute those who challenge destiny,
Those who are stronger than hatred
And who speak for the dead and the living.
All those whom despair has touched with its wing
Listen to the voice that never gives up,
The voice at morning, evening, midnight
When London is being bombed for the hundredth time.

Friends without faces, hands held out
Across this measureless distance,
You speak and we listen,

You live and we were about to die;
For we know from now on that one can die of shame.
Ici Londres, Parla Londra, London calling,
We are listening, we, the shipwrecked,
We who are gnawed by doubts and disquiet,
Crouched in the shadow and silent until we rage,
When London is being bombed for the hundredth time.

You who speak, you who call
Through the wind and the smoke and the blood,
You who appeal for our help towards our liberation,
You who are fighting that we may fight,
Ici Londres, Parla Londra, London calling,
Contre nous de la tyrannie l'étendard sanglant est levé,
Entendez-vous,
We are breathing, hearing, listening:
London is being bombed for the hundredth time.

London is being bombed for the hundredth time:
Nothing is lost, you are awake,
When Big Ben and the city's bells
State that it is exactly midnight,
That it is the hour of new courage,
Melbourne listens, and Ottawa,
The Cape, Calcutta, Auckland,
All the cities of the world,
All the villages of France
And Paris, too.

NIGHT VOYAGE

TRANSLATED FROM THE GERMAN OF
HEINRICH HEINE

The sea was high, the half-moon peeped
Through dark clouds timidly,
And, as we mounted on the skiff,
Our company numbered three.

The water splashed to the beat of the oar
With dull monotony;
White-crested waves came surging up
And spattered us all three.

She stood on the skiff, so slim, so pale,
And so unflinchingly,
Like a marble statue from foreign lands,
Diana's image, she.

And now the moon is entirely hid,
The wind blows cold and dree;
High, of a sudden, above our heads
A cry rings piercingly.

'Twas the cry of a white and spectral gull:
Like a warning prophecy
It rang, that sinister, evil cry,
And we were afraid, all three.

Am I a-fevered? Is yonder a ghost?
Or some midnight phantasy?
Am I mocked by a dream? Ah, what a dream,
What ghastly buffoonery!

Ghastly buffoonery! I dream
That salvation comes through Me:
That 'tis I who bear the heavy Cross
With steadfast loyalty.

Poor Beauty, she is sore distressed:
'Tis I who shall set her free
From shame and sin, from pain and want
And the world's obscenity.

Beauty distressed, ah, do not shrink
From this bitter pharmacy:
'Tis I myself who award thee death,
Though my heart shall die with thee.

Ah, buffoonery, cruel dream,
Madness and lunacy!
The night's agape, the ocean shrieks –
O God, ah, succour me!

Ah, succour me, all-merciful God!
What is't that falls in the sea?
Oh, hear, oh, hear, all-merciful God,
Adonai, hear my plea!

The sun arose, we put for land;
There was blossom on every tree!
And as we descended from the skiff,
Two were our company.

Norman Cameron 1905–1953

Norman Cameron was born in Bombay on 18 April 1905, the first of four children, three boys and a girl, born to the Reverend John Cameron MA, and his wife Isabel Macrae Cameron. John Cameron had been a chaplain in a Scots regiment in the Khyber pass and later gained a civil appointment in India. Isabel Macrae was the daughter of a widow who had been a friend of the Cameron family. They met when he was studying theology in Edinburgh, and corresponded for fifteen years before marrying.

The duties of a chaplain did not occupy all of John Cameron's time. He wrote articles for pocket money, although no samples have been preserved, and showing a concern for literary standards like that later displayed by his eldest son, refused to contribute to the *Encyclopaedia Britannica* when invited to do so (he was a student of the languages, religions, customs and coinage of the Middle East) on the grounds that the reference work was too poorly written.

There were brains on both sides of the family. Barbara MacIver, the poet's maternal great-grandmother, had been born a Macaulay, a relative of the Whig politician, historian and essayist. The poet's paternal grandmother, Ann Eliza Hunter, was a Hunter of Hunterston, the Ayrshire family that had produced the famous pair of brothers who were physicians and students of anatomy, William and John Hunter. Something of John Hunter's eccentric character may have been inherited by the poet. The *Encyclopaedia Britannica* describes Hunter as '... unconstrained, unbookish, sometimes crude though often vivid in his expression, and honest, unselfconscious and generous perhaps even to a fault.'

When Cameron's parents dedicated him to the God of the Church of Scotland through infant baptism, they named him John Norman, no doubt after his father and an uncle, a brother of his mother who had died at the age of eighteen as a cadet at Sandhurst.

Cameron's father rose in the civil ranks, eventually becoming senior presidency chaplain in Bombay. It is unlikely that

Cameron spent many of his early years in India. He and his brother Lewis, who was born in 1907, were sent to live with their maternal grandmother Catherine Macrae in Edinburgh, when still quite young. This arrangement did not work well.

For one thing, the grandmother showed a marked preference for the younger boy, then little more than a baby. She was also troubled by young Norman's verbal bluntness. Cameron's sister, Catherine Cameron Percival, writes: 'My grandmother was pretty and charming and generous and kind, but she was vain . . . and she liked people to flatter her. This was quite alien to Norman's soul, as he was a most direct person – and I really think he disliked her . . .' He felt so exiled in his grandmother's home that in later life he spoke of her with a harshness and vehemence he applied to no one else.

By 1913, the year in which Cameron's father died in India of a cerebral hemorrhage, brought on by congenital hypertension, Norman had been boarded with Bessie Walker Todd, who was a family friend and possibly a distant relation. His life with her seems to have been happy. He called her 'Muzz', as her own children did; and her son, Walker Todd, an architect and the father of Ruthven Todd, the poet and writer, became for him a special friend, a kind of spiritual anchor.

Cameron's formal education began when he was sent to Alton Burn, a small preparatory school on the golf course in Nairn where kinfolk lived. The school was Spartan by today's standards – austere and sparse furnishings, cold water for washing, large, draughty rooms, and much schoolwork. Dr Ray, the headmaster, with his small staff, introduced the young scholars to classical languages, mathematics, geography, literature and history. Cameron must have felt impressed by the master because he revisited the school and gave his former teacher a copy of his first book.

His precocity (no one recalls how he learned to read; it seemed to the family that he had taught himself at an early age), the education he received at home, and the instruction at Dr Ray's school combined to prepare Cameron to win a scholarship to Fettes College, Edinburgh, at the extraordinarily early age of eleven. (Boys usually entered Fettes at the age of fourteen.)

When Cameron entered the college, a stiff, stern routine

prevailed, the 'fag system' was in force, and rugby football played a large part in school life. The chaos spread by World War I also swept across the academic routine: teachers and former students went off to the trenches, German was banished from the curriculum, and students engaged in quasi-military drills and operations.

He was uncomfortable and unhappy at Fettes. His extre ne youth, his physical awkwardness and weakness, and his tendency to daydream combined to make him something of an outsider at the school. But he began to write at Fettes – serious poems, translations, prose sketches, and routine journalism for the school magazine, *The Fettesian*. Writing seems to have helped him become a part of the life of the school. G. P. S. Macpherson, a rugby player and scholar at the school and two years Cameron's senior, writes:

I remember Norman Cameron well, with his loose-jointed shambling gait and large head. He was a frail eleven-year-old as a new man [sic] in 1916, an inept fag, but protected by his defencelessness ... Rugger practices must have been pretty tough for him, and in his later years he probably was reprieved. Certainly I recall that when I was playing against the school before going up for the winter term of 1921 or 1922, he wrote the account for *The Fettesian*.

Eventually, 'Billiken', the nickname Cameron used as a pen name, became a regular contributor to *The Fettesian*. He also found some congenial and helpful spirits among the younger masters – Walter Sellar, who wrote light verse and co-authored the best-selling *1066 and All That*, became a life-long friend; and he probably had the run of the library of Dan Vaudrey, which included books that were disapproved of by more senior members of the staff – Joyce's *Portrait of the Artist as a Young Man*, Wyndham Lewis's *Tarr*, and others.

He played golf and chess, excelled at classics, but really distinguished himself through English verse. He won a Governor's Prize as well as the prize awarded for English verse in both 1922 and 1923. He also distinguished himself in another way: he probably spent more time at Fettes than any other boy in this century.

Cameron matriculated at Oriel College on 15 October 1924. He had been elected to the college that April on a classics exhibition worth £100 a year. He also held a Bible Clerkship, a kind of scholarship which required that he perform certain tasks of a religious nature. He carried out these duties in a characteristically memorable way. According to A. J. P. Taylor, the historian: 'Because he was a Bible Clerk, Norman was required to say grace before meals. Routinely, after the prayer, the Bible Clerk sat down with the rest of the scholars to eat. Often, because he was in a hurry to leave for a party, he would rattle off the prayer in his distinctive mutter, turn on his heel, and leave.'

Another undergraduate friend J. I. M. Stewart, better known by his pen name Michael Innes, recalls: 'He sometimes got drunk at inconvenient times – before having to read the lesson, for example, in the Oriel chapel. He is said on one occasion to have begun with the splendid words: "Here beginneth the fourth chapter of the Gospel according to St George"; the Provost barked at him from his stall: "John, boy, John"; but Norman majestically repeated what he had said and then went ahead.'

Oriel College was not exactly a haunt of the muses at that time, to use J. I. M. Stewart's phrase. For this reason, Cameron made his best friends elsewhere. Sir John Betjeman writes:

He was one of a group which was known in my world at Oxford as the 'Corpus Aesthetes'. They were John Aldridge, who was a painter even when at Oxford; Gilbert Armitage; Gabriele Toyne; Eric Shroeder and they spilled across the road to Oriel College and thus included Norman Cameron and Jack Yates . . . Norman was known as 'Wishy Cameron'. I can't think why unless it were that he was rather pale and quiet. He spoke little and had a hidden depth which sometimes appeared in a blunt statement.

He proved relatively prolific at Oxford, and as his friend of later years, James Reeves, has pointed out, his style became 'all but perfected as an undergraduate in the twenties.' In fact, the first ten poems in his 1957 *Collected Poems* appeared in the *Oxford Poetry* series of anthologies during the years from 1926 to 1928. Roy Fuller, considering only the contributions to *Oxford Poetry 1927*, writes: 'Even the undergraduate poetic brilliance of William Empson rather pales, I think, beside such an achievement.'

At Oxford Cameron at first seemed to be laying the ground-work for a rather traditional literary career. He delivered a paper on psychoanalysis and literature to a literary society, published poems and even a piece of fiction in the *Oxford Outlook*, and by 1926 was an assistant editor of the *Outlook*. It may have been his meeting with Laura Riding and Robert Graves at Oxford in 1927 that led him to question the value of this kind of activity. At any rate, it is a fact that after 1927 he no longer appears as active in literary societies or as holding edi-torial posts.

Laura Riding came to Oxford, accompanied by Robert Graves, to deliver a talk to a student group. It may be that Cameron instigated the invitation. In any case, he was certainly a member of the audience and became friendly with them after the proceedings. He visited with Riding and Graves at the headquarters of their press, The Seizin Press, at St Peter's Square, Hammersmith, in London. He also spent long vacations on the Continent, and it is probably through these travels, rather than through academic work, that he gained his excellent knowledge of German and French.

Cameron was never a dogged scholar and did not do par-ticularly well in his finals – taking a fourth class in Literae Humaniores. After Trinity term, that is in June 1928, he left Oxford for London. He found a studio at 49c British Grove in Chiswick, around the corner from St Peter's Square and the partners of The Seizin Press. A letter to John Aldridge, sugges-ting that they share the studio, brought the painter to London. A small inheritance temporarily set Cameron free from the need to earn a living, and he embarked on a kind of Bohemian existence.

Another one of those in the circle that gathered around Laura Riding and Robert Graves was a young New Zealander called Len Lye, then living on a barge on the Thames. He made batiks, designed decorations and covers for works issued by The Seizin Press, and eventually became best known as a pioneering maker of experimental animated films. He was a devotee of American jazz, and the sounds of Bix Beiderbecke or Red Nichols frequently rose from his barge. His impres-sions of Cameron succinctly characterize both men: 'Norman was a long-legged walking essence of poetry himself with a dry humour of marvellous wit and sociability. He would sit in a low arm chair, long legs crossed and waggle his foot while balancing his slipper, his toe caught under its tongue. His jokes would always conclude with a snigger down his long nose.'

Cameron, of course, maintained his older friendships, too. Walter Sellar and his wife, Hope, visited him in British Grove. She remembered him years later as '... a tall, pale, rather shaggy young man with a shy manner and very wide, friendly smile who treated us to vodka and rye whisky in his rooms in London one evening. I remember he had a vast double bed there! He was a most amusing and friendly person ... I remember his telling us of a recent camping trip with a girlfriend on the Continent, when their tent was blown down, and he pulled his trousers over both of them in an endeavour to keep warm.'

His way of life inevitably caused his mother some concern. She was a warm, gracious, generous woman who enjoyed entertaining his friends in Edinburgh. For years Alan Hodge, John Pudney, Dylan Thomas and others wore sweaters she had knitted for them. But she was anxious about her son's way of life in London, and he did, at times, get into scrapes. J. I. M. Stewart remembers: 'He was lazily amused by his discomfitures and even catastrophes. I envied him his power to chuckle ruefully and forgivingly over small episodes and misadventures I'd myself have been ashamed of and alarmed by. It wasn't exactly a matter of his being intellectually detached from and sardonically observant of himself. He was very open to suffering, including his own, and went around in this lumbering unassuming carapace about which there was something very attractive.'

One of these catastrophes involved the partners of The Seizin Press. Laura Riding jumped out of a window, and required an emergency operation on her spine. Robert Graves separated from his wife and children, and eventually, he and Riding left England and established their press in Majorca. These events strained Cameron's financial resources, and he took a job as an education officer with the Colonial Service in Nigeria.

In a letter to Laura Riding written on board ship bound for Nigeria, Cameron gives one of his reasons for accepting the post in Africa: 'I thought that it was meeting too many people whom I loved or liked that was dissipating my slight energy in London. I certainly haven't met anybody loveable or likeable on this ship so I hope for good results.'

The results were not, in fact, good. The climate disagreed with him, and he began to suffer from fevers, much as he had at Fettes when faced with anxieties over exams. In addition, the work proved tedious and his co-workers uncongenial. He found that he began to dream with some frequency of being with his friends in Majorca. He wrote:

I woke up at about 6.30 this morning when it was sunny and misty and cool and went to sleep and dreamed about being in Spain with you chaps, in a large house with long solid tables, very big rooms with smoked hams or something hanging up. There were some Spaniards there, one of them being a dominant woman with whom we were all just having a meal, I think, not staying there. There was lots of good food about. It was a fine dream . . .

Although he had agreed to stay in Nigeria for three years, he left for Deyá, Majorca, after having served only eighteen months. According to Robert Graves, Cameron went to Majorca intending to 'devote himself to pure literature'. The change of scene and the reunion with his friends must have agreed with him because he began to build and equip a house there. He also became involved in some of the writing projects that Riding and Graves relied on for money. He worked at a rewriting of *The Pickwick Papers* that was intended to parallel Graves's revision of *David Copperfield*. He never finished this task, however, and returned to London in 1933 with Elfriede Faust, a German woman he had met in Majorca. They married on 17 June 1933, at the registry office in Hammersmith and set up housekeeping in the studio in British Grove. Elfriede Faust was then twenty-four years old and, according to Len Lye, 'a beautiful golden-haired one'. Cameron's 'A Visit to the Dead' is a satiric, backward glance at the more precious and petty aspects of the literary life as he had experienced it in Majorca.

Back in London, he rapidly discovered a congenial way of making a living and began to establish himself as a poet. He became an advertising copywriter with J. Walter Thompson, an American advertising agency with English offices in Bush

House in the Strand. 'Norman enjoyed copywriting,' Robert Graves writes, 'and brought to it the same passionate exactitude that he applied in his poems. It amused him to find out all he could about the manufacture of ice-cream, cheese-spreads, tonic wines, or whatever it might be, and then set his precise imagination to the task of selling them.' His precise imagination at times turned light-heartedly ghoulish. Len Lye remembers that Cameron 'invented the horrible idea of frightening the be-jesus out of all hypochondriacs by showing how bile acids ate away carpets and rugs to leave great holes where the fancy patterns had been.'

Cameron's most successful campaign was called Night Starvation, a 'disease' which could be cured by drinking a glass of hot Horlick's Malted Milk last thing at night. This became the basis for a parody among Cameron and his friends – 'Night Custard', a punning expansion of the poet's initials and a pun on the name of a popular artist, McKnight Kauffer. Ruthven Todd, who along with Dylan Thomas, Len Lye, and others contributed to this serial myth, recalls that 'Night Custard' could be 'anything from the guck that gathers under beds to a kind of stew of squashed slugs. Alas that I cannot now recall the intricate details of the various campaigns which we planned as promotion for this disgusting subject. Norman, as might have been expected, was the best at inventing really revolting slogans and all kinds of possible uses for the revolting substance, from hair cream to vaginal jelly.'

Cameron's attitude toward copywriting was, as James Reeves has pointed out, basically cynical. But he also maintained standards and thought of the work as a way of keeping fit for poetry. His poems began to appear with increasing frequency in periodicals in the early thirties. Some appeared in *The Listener*, but most found a home in the pages of Geoffrey Grigson's *New Verse*, arguably the most distinguished poetry journal of the period. His first book, *The Winter House and Other Poems*, was published by Dent in 1935. These publications established his reputation among poets if not with the general public.

The pages of *New Verse* also contained the only statement of principles on poetry Cameron seems to have ever composed. Grigson sent a questionnaire to forty poets and published their responses in the magazine. His questions and Cameron's terse, witty answers to them are given here in full:

1. *Do you intend your poetry to be useful to yourself or others?* Neither. I write a poem because I think it wants to be written.

2. *Do you think there can now be a use for narrative poetry?* I don't know.

3. *Do you wait for a spontaneous impulse before writing a poem; if so, is this impulse verbal or visual?* (a) Yes. (b) Neither; first impulse comes from a vague sensation, as if somewhere at the back of my head.

4. *Have you been influenced by Freud and how do you regard him?* (a) No. I haven't read any writings by Freud since I was a schoolboy ten years ago. (b) I regard him as I do, say, Major Douglas, [the father of Social Credit in political economy, Ezra Pound's idol] – i.e. for all I know his doctrines are irrefutable, but I don't care to study them.

5. *Do you take your stand with any political or politico-economic party or creed?* I believe that Communism is necessary and good, but I'm not eager for it. To act, from a feeling of moral compulsion, as if I were eager for it would be hysterical.

6. *As a poet, what distinguishes you, do you think, from an ordinary man?* Lack of interest in ordinary human, masculine activities, such as sport, learning and making a career. In so far as I am interested in these, the less I am a poet.

This attitude toward poetry helps make clear the reasons for the relatively small number of poems Cameron wrote. He produced poems only when he felt compelled to do so. In a way, his advertising copy and commissioned prose translations constitute the equivalent of the dead-wood that causes some other poets' published works to bulk.

From 1933 until the outbreak of World War II, Cameron's life found a pattern, a routine. Copywriting earned him enough money to afford the convivial life he enjoyed – throwing lavish parties and entertaining writers and artists, what he called his 'witty worm friends', with pub crawls. Because of his job, he had no financial motive for pursuing literature as a career and so produced few reviews and rarely was tempted to try his hand at prose. (He apparently wrote a film script, never produced and now lost, about a women's revolt in Nigeria.)

He wrote poems when they came to him and worked on his translations of Rimbaud's verse in much the same way, fitfully, when the spirit moved him. In fact, his method of composition for original poems and translations was the same, and early established at Fettes through the translation of classical poets. 'As I was trained to do when writing Latin and Greek translations at school,' he wrote, 'I put down lines on the page about where I think they're going to come in.'

At times, Cameron's professional and convivial lives met in one person. William Sansom worked with him at J. Walter Thompson and also experienced his way of life after hours, particularly in a favorite wine shop, Henekey's in the Strand. Sansom has recorded his memories in affectionate detail:

At the advertising office, my room was changed. I was put in an office-for-two with a strange tall man with an uncombed mop of hair, and a long woolen tie. He came in with a kind of breezy, serious gusto, carrying a lot of dangerous-looking thin books, private stuff, poetry. After an affable greeting or two, he turned to write copy about a liver-medicine on the bright yellow paper provided for such purposes. I returned to dealing with a nail-polish remover, literally only, but meanwhile stole a glance or two at the stranger's visionary pale eyes and his suit, which seemed to be made of hair. I had seen nobody like this before; or if I had, had averted my smooth little eyes.

At midday this man suddenly turned and said: 'How about some gudfud?' As a new boy I was prepared to agree to anything. But within a couple of hours I had understood exactly what Norman Cameron meant by his soon-to-be-well-known invitation to good food, had met my first poet and been astounded that he laughed and drank, ate and enjoyed life like other people. It was the first of many such lunches. Years later I asked him what on earth had prompted him to bear the company of someone who could only talk of Louis Armstrong and the like, and scarcely understood half he could have said. He answered that it was because in the morning I brought into the office a breath of brandy from the night before – I was helping to run a nightclub at the time – and that this was invigorating . . .

When the office closed we would often walk along to a wine shop where goodish cheap hock was served on heavy wood tables, and there I met a number of Norman's friends – an astounded cherub called Thomas, a clerkly-looking fellow called Gascoyne, egg-domed

Len Lye like an ascetic coster in his raffish cap, and many others whose names I cannot immediately remember but who, with hock and words, signed and resigned this new lease to my life. What impressed me most was that, unlike certain other writers *manqués* back in the office, they did not discuss literary theory or whine about their souls and sensitivities – they made up things there and then, grabbed down stories and myths from the air, wrote down doggerel and verse . . . Until those times I had still thought of a poet as a cartoonist's poet, a sort of gangling sissy dancing among lambs in spring.

Cameron's marriage to Elfriede Faust seems to have been without a strong foundation. His family suspected that they married largely to provide her with an opportunity to become a British subject. In any case, his way of life no doubt strained the relationship. They separated, and she died on 6 May 1936, at the age of twenty-six. It then became clear that she had for some time suffered from tuberculosis, the disease that killed her. Cameron remained friendly with her parents and her sister Thea, and visited them in Germany in 1937 with Antonia White, the novelist who worked with him at J. Walter Thompson.

Franco's fascist revolution against the Spanish Republic caused people throughout the world to take up political positions. Cameron was clearly identified with the left, thought of himself as a Socialist of sorts, had friends in the Independent Labour Party, but could not bring himself to volunteer to go to Spain. As he had written in *New Verse* about Communism, he felt that for him to take such an action would be 'hysterical'. Nonetheless, he clearly struggled with the question. He explained his position in his contribution to Laura Riding's *The World and Ourselves*, a collection of replies to a letter asking for views on the relation of 'inside people' to 'outside people' and the world:

Well, then, here is the human situation: socially unjust, economically mad, the cause of a huge amount of unnecessary human misery, the product of the base human impulses – different kinds of people choose to deplore it in different terms, and I agree with all of them.

Should I, then, try to do anything to change this human situation? Yes, provided I can do so without acting hysterically. By acting hysterically I mean identifying myself with people and causes with whom or which I have no real identity. Thus, although all the terms of abuse for the human situation that I have listed above are relatively true, I belong to none of the various kinds of people who have a natural inclination to use these various terms; I should, therefore, be acting hysterically if I were to act as they do, join in their political or economic groups and activities – for example, going to fight for the Spanish Government.

My refusal to do this last leads me, of course, to ask myself whether what I have written so far is merely an excuse for being selfish, cowardly or lazy. But I don't believe that I am selfish or cowardly; and, as for laziness, that can be a fault, but it can also be an avoidance of hysteria.

Clearly he was not politically naive; but neither was he what Wyndham Lewis called a 'Revolutionary Simpleton': he found no comfort in a future of political gangsterism and industrial feudalism. As Robert Graves put it: 'Decency of behaviour was what he demanded. Neither the Nazis, nor (later) the Bolsheviks, came up to his standards, so he felt free to say exactly what he thought of them.'

Laura Riding and Robert Graves introduced Cameron to Catherine de la Roche, a Russian of a Huguenot family, who then worked in the scenario department of Korda's London Films, at Easter in 1938. They soon became frequent, if not constant, companions and married on 3 September 1938. She writes in a letter to me: 'One of the first serious things he confided in me was his fervent desire to justify a "gift of compassion". This was toward the end of one of our early outings, dinner at the Café Royal, and I can still hear the words: "A poet's talent *is* important and if I'm a poet I hope to live up to this, but being a good poet isn't my greatest ambition. If I have a really important gift, I think it's compassion."'

During his service as a civilian propagandist attached to military units during World War II, he had opportunities to exercise this 'gift of compassion'. Many of the people he met during the war experienced a kind of healing power they associated with his presence.

The poet and painter Oswell Blakeston was then a conscientious objector who felt 'psychically drenched in blood'. He recalls that after a few minutes spent with Cameron '. . . one felt one was in an Edwardian garden and one expected to see a waiter, in a white coat, appear at any moment to serve chilled champagne.' Marie-Christine and Robert Mengin, exiles from France in England to whom Cameron inscribed his poem, 'The Invader', felt something of the same power. Mengin wrote in his *No Laurels for De Gaulle*: 'Norman was a huge chap, six feet six in height, careless in his dress, hair never combed, and with the politest, most aristocratic manners. On our arrival, he welcomed us as if we were guests long and impatiently awaited. He had such a gift for hospitality and was so gracious that one was warmed by the mere offering of a cigarette or of a chair.' Similarly, Doris Temple, who worked with Cameron in the German Section at Woburn Abbey early in the war, recalls: 'He did not always arrive on time for a meeting. He would come, filling up the whole doorway for a moment while he ran his aristocratic fingers through his hair, apologizing in his short, jerky speech: "I'm – sorry – chaps – but . . ." Then it wouldn't matter, and the chairman would say, "Ah! here's Norman," and everyone would feel warm and good-natured . . . It seems to me that everyone had affection for him and that when he appeared, people would show a side of themselves better than they knew and that the world became a kinder place – less sad – when someone said, "Ah! here's Norman."'

The war took him to North Africa, Italy, and finally Austria. He wrote radio dialogues called 'Kurt und Willy' intended to undermine German faith in Nazi propaganda; he wrote passes that promised safe conduct to the bearer and that urged German troops to surrender; and he worked on a number of newspapers that variously appeared in German and English. He is said to have considered the war 'a sordid interruption of one's personal life', but felt compelled to suppress his gloom or anger whenever these threatened to surface in an effort to keep up the morale of those around him.

His second marriage had been strained by what Catherine de la Roche considered conflicting loyalties. She resented his financial support of Dylan Thomas, Len Lye, and other impecunious friends. She also admits to having been jealous of other women. Separated for long periods by the war, the marriage ended in divorce.

Shortly before leaving England, he was able to finish his translations of Rimbaud and see them through the press. In 1942 The Hogarth Press published a small book of poems, entitled *Work in Hand*, by Cameron, Robert Graves, and Alan Hodge, another member of the Graves and Riding circle who collaborated with Graves in *The Long Week-End* (1940) and *The Reader Over Your Shoulder* (1943).

Cameron wrote a handful of poems during the war. On 10 April 1944 he sent three of these, 'Green, Green is El Aghir', 'Via Maestranza', and 'Steep Stone Steps', to John Lehmann for possible publication in *New Writing* along with the following letter:

Here are three travel-sketch kind of poems, in case you want to print them for your magazine ...

In a letter I got from you some time ago, you said something about living in mud and cold. I'm afraid I can't claim to be suffering any hardship, except lack of sheets. I live in comfort. I did do a trip recently to a comparatively forward area, and there I was more comfortable than ever, since soldiers in the field look after themselves as well as they can, when they can. In a Polish mess, for example, I had the best meal since 1940 – all made out of ordinary British rations, but quite unrecognizable.

What else? I'm beginning, despite all this comfort, to feel the effects of exile. As Robert Graves remarked about his stay in Egypt, one can live on one's hump only for so long, and my hump is not large. I want to see some friends again. I'm getting rather rich here – one can't spend much of one's pay – so when I get home, in a few months, perhaps, the way the Russians are now going, I'll stand you and some other people a good dinner.

He was not to rejoin London friends for some time to come, the way the Russians were then rumoured to be going notwithstanding. As the waste of life went on, as a way of life was eradicated, he drank more heavily. His unit once put on a skit containing light-hearted commentary on its members. He was described as 'Always misty/On Lacrimae Christi'. In 1945 he suffered from what he later described as fits of 'melancholia', bouts of depression he tried to shake off by visiting various churches, only to be inevitably disappointed by the proceedings and to hastily leave.

When he returned briefly to England, he visited John Betjeman who remembered him at the time as 'content *and* at a loss'. He never satisfactorily reestablished himself in post-war London.

In October 1946 he decided to work again with the occupation forces in Vienna. He wrote James Reeves from Calais:

I've been held up here for a day – no train to Villach until this evening. The military authorities do their best, I must say, to make one comfortable and cheerful: loads of cigarettes, and chocolate, at less than pre-war prices – and, of course, rich army food which I find that I cannot stomach after a year of comparatively spare civilian living. The whole camp consists of Nissen huts amongst cinders, but the huts have little curtains in the window, and there is a cinema – showing, of course, a bum British film, but with remarkable bright blue plaster pillars erected in front of the corrugated iron. The young chap I'm travelling with – an Englishman, but he has spent so many years in Italy and Germany that he is alternately Italian and German – complained that the place had no soul. I told him that the little checked curtains and the blue pillars are full of soul.

In Vienna he met an Austrian journalist, Gretl Bajardi, and they made plans to marry. He began looking for work in England by writing to old friends in the advertising business. Eventually, he was hired by Stanhope Shelton as a copywriter with the English advertising agency of Mather and Crowther. He and Gretl settled in what had been his last pre-war address in London, 7 Queen's Gate Place, and he tried to reestablish his pre-war life. Soon people were flowing through the flat for parties, he and Dylan Thomas hauled Tosco Fyvel out of the offices of *Tribune* for a pub crawl, and he and Gretl enjoyed lavish dinners in restaurants. His poems and translations appeared in *New Writing*, *The Poetry Review*, *Quarto*, a broadside James Reeves founded in 1950, and *Botteghe Oscura*.

The deaths of Cameron's mother and brother, Lewis, signal his own decline. He had long wanted to translate the poems of François Villon. He considered that the inheritances he expected from the estates of his mother and brother would provide him with sufficient income to give up his job and concentrate on the Villon translations, as well as earning money through commissioned translations of prose works. He decided to borrow against these expected inheritances in order to put this plan into action immediately. Doing so required that he take a physical examination. As a result, it was discovered that he suffered from extremely high blood pressure.

This finding precipitated a flurry of events. Doctors decided that the blood pressure called for immediate treatment. They first changed his diet: Gretl now prepared special dishes for him – baking salt-free bread, for instance – after her day's work at the BBC. It was at this time that he confided to friends that he wished he had met and married Gretl years before. The diet produced no effect on his obstinate hypertension.

He was next referred to a psychoanalyst to determine if the high blood pressure was a psychosomatic symptom. He paid four or five visits to Dr Ian Chrichton-Miller, a well-known analyst and a fellow Scot. He seems to have enjoyed these sessions thoroughly. For instance, he met Charles Beauclerc for drinks after one such session. 'Very interesting,' Cameron announced. 'We talked about the difference between lust and love. Think it's lust with him.' James Reeves once asked Cameron if the analyst had taught him anything. 'He said he had not,' Reeves reports, 'but that he felt the analyst had learned something from him.' After these few visits the doctor was satisfied that the hypertension had other than emotional roots and should be treated in another way – a decision which worked to Cameron's disadvantage, it may be, as it placed him under the surgeon's knife.

He underwent a sympathectomy at Charing Cross Hospital in 1950, lost his senses for a time, and was given up for dead by some of his friends. He survived, however, and in a few weeks returned to Queen's Gate Place. He told Robert Mengin that the effect of the operation was comparable to a terrible blow on the head with a sledge hammer.

Shortly before this operation, but when he was by no means in good health, his wife received a letter from a nun in Austria, a friend of hers, who had greatly impressed Cameron by her generous and cheerful aid to the needy of Vienna. The Sister had learned that Cameron was not a Catholic, and from her point of view, worse, a divorced man. In the eyes of mother Church, and so in her's, they were not married, but were living in sin. 'No bells will toll for you when you die,' she warned.

Expecting Cameron to find the letter funny, his wife read it to him. To her astonishment, instead of laughing, he looked unusually serious and said: 'We'll go and see Father Carter at Oxford tomorrow.' She protested that she thought the letter would amuse him, but he would not be dissuaded from his decision – apparently convinced his conversion would comfort her. The next day, they took the train to Oxford where they met his undergraduate friend, Douglas Carter, who had become a Roman Catholic priest, and together they planned his conversion. John Aldridge, who later married Cameron's widow, said that Cameron had converted for the best of reasons – for love.

Sickness was not all he had to struggle against while striving to finish his Villon translations. His flat was struck by fire in 1951, and he had to endure the sight of his library destroyed. He wrote to James Reeves on 26 May:

Yes, it was a real fire all right and a damned bad one . . . cost us all our decent furniture, or nearly, pictures – including that lovely Chinese one – and, worst of all, all the books I valued. But nearly all my manuscripts escaped, beds, bedding, clothes, kitchen gear, etc., so it might have been worse. For that matter, we might well have been roasted ourselves – Alan [Hodge], who was spending the night with us – woke up just in time – but we are intact except that Gretl got her nose and ears a little scorched.

It's very good of you to ask us to Weymouth, but this is not a good time. I am staying with the Hodges – the flat is too dirty to work in – and Gretl is sleeping in the flat above ours keeping an eye on things. There are huge holes in the living-room and ceiling, but the landlord's engineer hopes to get to work soon and have the place repaired in a few weeks – very good, if true, for the room is burnt out to the bricks, not even a picture-nail left – and after that we can start reconstructing our abode.

Never get too much attached to property. 'Lives are more important than things,' as the chief pilot said on the occasion when mother was pulled through the port-hole of a blazing 'plane nearly two years ago. There's fire in our family.

       Love to both from us both,

         Norman

In a postscript he added: 'The reason why I've been so long in answering is that I've been toiling hard to catch up with my translation schedule. I now have a German book of 90,000 complicated words to translate in a month.'

Spells of concentrated work were offset by parties and visits to friends. But he never fully recovered from the operation he had undergone and appeared to friends to be obviously failing. At Easter, 1953, Cameron and his wife stayed with James and Mary Reeves in Chalfont. Reeves writes: 'It was as delightful as ever, but Norman was weaker than we supposed.' Cameron died of a cerebral hemorrhage at his home on 20 April 1953, two days after his forty-eighth birthday. An anonymous tribute, probably by Alan Hodge, appeared in *The Times* on Thursday, 23 April: 'Norman Cameron was a man who made integrity a gay and entertaining virtue, and the world will now be a poorer place for all who knew him.'

He was buried at London's Brompton Cemetery following the celebration of a requiem Mass attended by his family, his friends, and representatives of both the French and Italian ambassadors. Something of his Puckish spirit dominated these solemn proceedings, as William Sansom noticed: 'I went to his funeral ... which was sad and funny, the holy water being brought by a priest in a bottle of Eno's Fruit Salts – which Norman would have giggled at very much.'

An unofficial poet's wake was held for him in New York when news of his death reached Ruthven Todd and Dylan Thomas there. They met at the White Horse, a Greenwich Village bar, then the haunt of teamsters and longshoremen, peppered with writers and painters, and took turns reading Cameron's poems aloud to what Todd has described as 'a remarkably appreciative audience'.

His simple, almost Spartan gravestone bears this inscription: 'John Norman Cameron 1905–1953'.

WARREN HOPE

Variants

As mentioned in the Note on page 20, Alan Hodge incorporated Cameron's final preferences in his edition of *The Collected Poems of Norman Cameron 1905–1953* (The Hogarth Press, 1957), which is the text followed for the relevant poems in this edition. A full list of variants, many of which would be punctuational minutiae, is inappropriate in an edition intended for reading rather than as a scholarly work. We list here only the more interesting or significant departures from the three earlier collections published in Cameron's lifetime: *The Winter House and Other Poems* (Dent, 1935), *Work in Hand* (The Hogarth Press, 1942) and *Forgive Me, Sire* (Fore Publications, 1950).

Pretty Maids all in a Row

The epigraph '(From a hand-book of advice to travellers)' appeared in *Oxford Poetry 1927* but not in *The Winter House*.

Decapitation of Is

Alan Hodge followed the *Oxford Poetry 1927* text. The version in *The Winter House* is:

> We tried one day to execute old Is,
> For his predicative, Protean vis-
> Age had annoyed us. But there was this check,
> None could discover the dividing neck
> Between Here-Is and There-Is, these and those.
> 'Strike here,' said One, and pointed at his toes.
> 'Strike there,' said Two. But what he meant by there,
> His pointing finger proved, was old Is' hair.
> Meanwhile, Is' face was working horribly,
> So that a sudden fear made us agree
> To give the business up. In any case
> We had not aimed to turn him into Was.

From a Woman to a Greedy Lover

Line 3: 'wrack' as in *Work in Hand*; 'rack' in *Forgive Me, Sire*.

The Wanton's Death

Lines 9–10 appear in both *Work in Hand* and *Forgive Me, Sire* as:

> She, to both quarters native, round them sporting.
> At length each suitor found a specious refuge,

Line 13: 'And' as in *Work in Hand*; 'Then' in *Forgive Me, Sire*.

The Invader

In *Forgive Me, Sire* the poem is dedicated: '(For Marie-Christine and Robert Mengin)'.

Green, Green is El Aghir

In *Forgive Me, Sire* the title is 'El Aghir'. There are also the following variants:
Line 1: 'bags and crates' for 'crates and sacks'
Line 10: 'facets' for 'faces'
Line 17: 'creed' for 'faith'

A Hook for Leviathan

In *Forgive Me, Sire* there are the following variants:
Line 1: 'Ah' for 'Why', 'Hook' for 'hook'
Line 8: 'accomplished' for 'completed'
Line 12: 'We'd' for 'We'll'
Line 15: 'found' for 'learnt'

Bibliography

Works by Norman Cameron in chronological order

Collections of Poetry

The Winter House and Other Poems, J. M. Dent & Sons, 1935.
Work in Hand, The Hogarth Press, 1942, The New Hogarth Library Vol. VI; with Alan Hodge and Robert Graves.
Forgive Me, Sire, Fore Publications, 1950.
Forgive Me, Sire, Alan Swallow (USA), 1950.
The Collected Poems of Norman Cameron 1905–1953, The Hogarth Press, 1957; with an introduction by Robert Graves.
The Complete Poems of Norman Cameron, Robert L. Barth (USA), 1985; edited and introduced by Warren Hope.

Verse Translations

Selected Verse Poems of Arthur Rimbaud, The Hogarth Press, 1942.
Soupault, Philippe: *Ode to Bombed London*, Editions Edmond Charlot (Algiers), 1944.
Rimbaud, Arthur: *A Season in Hell*, John Lehmann, 1949; with drawings by Keith Vaughan.
Villon, François: *Poems*, Jonathan Cape, 1952.

Prose Translations: A Selection

Voltaire: *Candide, or Optimism*, Hamish Hamilton, 1947.
Balzac, Honoré de: *Cousin Pons*, Hamish Hamilton, 1950.
Baudelaire, Charles: *My Heart Laid Bare and Other Prose Writings*, George Weidenfeld & Nicolson, 1950.
Kérenyi, Károlyi: *The Gods of the Greeks*, Thames & Hudson, 1951.
Bergengruen, Werner: *A Matter of Conscience*, Thames & Hudson, 1952.
Beyle, Marie Henri: *To the Happy Few: Selected Letters of Stendhal*, John Lehmann, 1952.
Constant, Benjamin: *Cécile*, John Lehmann, 1952.
Ivanov, V. I.: *Freedom and the Tragic Life*, Harvill Press, 1952.
Triolet, Elsa: *The Inspector of Ruins*, George Weidenfeld & Nicolson, 1952.
Deleuze, Bernard: *Vagabond of the Andes*, Jonathan Cape, 1953.
Hitler, Adolf: *Table Talk 1941–1944*, George Weidenfeld & Nicolson, 1953; translated with R. H. Stevens.
Murger, Henry: *Vie de Bohème*, The Folio Society, 1960.

Index of Titles and First Lines

(Titles are in italics)